BREAKFAST CEREAL

Edible

Series Editor: Andrew F. Smith

EDIBLE is a revolutionary series of books dedicated to food and drink that explores the rich history of cuisine. Each book reveals the global history and culture of one type of food or beverage.

Already published

Apple Erika Janik, *Avocado* Jeff Miller, *Banana* Lorna Piatti-Farnell, *Barbecue* Jonathan Deutsch and Megan J. Elias, *Beans* Nathalie Rachel Morris, *Beef* Lorna Piatti-Farnell, *Beer* Gavin D. Smith, *Berries* Heather Arndt Anderson, *Biscuits and Cookies* Anastasia Edwards, *Brandy* Becky Sue Epstein, *Bread* William Rubel, *Breakfast Cereal* Kathryn Cornell Dolan, *Cabbage* Meg Muckenhoupt, *Cake* Nicola Humble, *Caviar* Nichola Fletcher, *Champagne* Becky Sue Epstein, *Cheese* Andrew Dalby, *Chillies* Heather Arndt Anderson, *Chocolate* Sarah Moss and Alexander Badenoch, *Cocktails* Joseph M. Carlin, *Coconut* Constance L. Kirker and Mary Newman, *Cod* Elisabeth Townsend, *Coffee* Jonathan Morris, *Corn* Michael Owen Jones, *Curry* Colleen Taylor Sen, *Dates* Nawal Nasrallah, *Doughnut* Heather Delancey Hunwick, *Dumplings* Barbara Gallani, *Edible Flowers* Constance L. Kirker and Mary Newman, *Edible Insects* Gina Louise Hunter, *Eggs* Diane Toops, *Fats* Michelle Phillipov, *Figs* David C. Sutton, *Foie Gras* Norman Kolpas, *Game* Paula Young Lee, *Gin* Lesley Jacobs Solmonson, *Hamburger* Andrew F. Smith, *Herbs* Gary Allen, *Herring* Kathy Hunt, *Honey* Lucy M. Long, *Hot Dog* Bruce Kraig, *Hummus* Harriet Nussbaum, *Ice Cream* Laura B. Weiss, *Jam, Jelly and Marmalade* Sarah B. Hood, *Lamb* Brian Yarvin, *Lemon* Toby Sonneman, *Lobster* Elisabeth Townsend, *Melon* Sylvia Lovegren, *Milk* Hannah Velten, *Moonshine* Kevin R. Kosar, *Mushroom* Cynthia D. Bertelsen, *Mustard* Demet Güzey, *Nuts* Ken Albala, *Offal* Nina Edwards, *Olive* Fabrizia Lanza, *Onions and Garlic* Martha Jay, *Oranges* Clarissa Hyman, *Oyster* Carolyn Tillie, *Pancake* Ken Albala, *Pasta and Noodles* Kantha Shelke, *Pickles* Jan Davison, *Pie* Janet Clarkson, *Pineapple* Kaori O'Connor, *Pizza* Carol Helstosky, *Pomegranate* Damien Stone, *Pork* Katharine M. Rogers, *Potato* Andrew F. Smith, *Pudding* Jeri Quinzio, *Rice* Renee Marton, *Rum* Richard Foss, *Saffron* Ramin Ganeshram, *Salad* Judith Weinraub, *Salmon* Nicolaas Mink, *Sandwich* Bee Wilson, *Sauces* Maryann Tebben, *Sausage* Gary Allen, *Seaweed* Kaori O'Connor, *Shrimp* Yvette Florio Lane, *Soda and Fizzy Drinks* Judith Levin, *Soup* Janet Clarkson, *Spices* Fred Czarra, *Sugar* Andrew F. Smith, *Sweets and Candy* Laura Mason, *Tea* Helen Saberi, *Tequila* Ian Williams, *Tomato* Clarissa Hyman, *Truffle* Zachary Nowak, *Vanilla* Rosa Abreu-Runkel, *Vodka* Patricia Herlihy, *Water* Ian Miller, *Whiskey* Kevin R. Kosar, *Wine* Marc Millon, *Yoghurt* June Hersh

Breakfast Cereal

A Global History

Kathryn Cornell Dolan

REAKTION BOOKS

To Olivia

Published by Reaktion Books Ltd
Unit 32, Waterside
44–48 Wharf Road
London N1 7UX, UK
www.reaktionbooks.co.uk

First published 2023
Copyright © Kathryn Cornell Dolan 2023

Printed and bound in India by Replika Press Pvt. Ltd

A catalogue record for this book is available from the British Library

ISBN 978 1 78914 695 0

Contents

Introduction

Let's start with a question: where did the breakfast cereals we all grew up enjoying – cereals like granola and Cheerios – come from? As I began researching this topic, I noticed the prevalence of breakfast cereals – ready-to-eat as well as warm porridges – throughout history and across the globe. While porridges are truly ancient, cold breakfast cereals are a more recent and decidedly American development, though one that quickly expanded to the rest of the world. The breakfast cereals imagined in the nineteenth century in some ways bear little resemblance to the cereals lining the shelves of grocery stores and supermarkets in the twenty-first century, but they are connected in their deep history.

The story of cereal began around 10,000 years ago, and in several regions of the world, with the advent of agriculture, which centred around grains such as wheat, rice and maize – also known as corn. The development of ceramic pots allowed grains to be cooked over a fire, revolutionizing how people could prepare their grains and making them much easier to consume. Harvested grains could also be stored safely, and this would have lasting consequences for numerous global cultures. The porridges made from these and other great grains are as storied as the regions and peoples that have been preparing them since antiquity.

It's always breakfast time somewhere, 1935, colour lithograph.

In the second half of the nineteenth century, in the United States, a series of entrepreneurs and food reformers – many of whom were connected to religious institutions – created a new kind of cereal: cold breakfast cereal. In the industry's early days, the diet innovators who went on to develop the cereals we recognize today – Kellogg's Corn Flakes, Post Grape-Nuts (a wheat bran cereal broken into small nuggets) and Quaker Oats, among others – were largely centred in a few small cities in the U.S. Midwest. Since that time, food scientists have worked to improve on these original recipes, developing new flavour combinations and, most notably, adding sugar. Breakfast cereals acquired new shapes

William Hemsley, *Porridge*, 1893, oil on canvas.

and sizes as well, once machines had been developed that could 'puff' grains. Already a convenient food, cold cereal was made healthier and even more appealing to consumers through the addition of vitamins, discovered in the early twentieth century.

The development of cold breakfast cereal, interestingly, coincided with a trend among world cuisines to increasingly style themselves after the USA, and this movement grew stronger in the second half of the twentieth century. As Rachel Laudan observes: 'American cuisine now included milk, vegetables, and fruit as well as bread, beef, fat, and sugar. Meals were based on hot or cold cereal for breakfast, soup and a sandwich for lunch, and meat and two vegetables for dinner.'[1] U.S. cuisine in general, and breakfast cereal in particular, has been influencing international gastronomic trends ever since.

Cereal with blueberries and mint.

Gerrit Dou, *Woman Eating Porridge*, c. 1632–7, oil on panel.

One example of this cereal-related impact on food cultures and traditions can be seen by taking a close look at the development of breakfast foods – including ready-to-eat cereals – in Italy. This nation, famous for its cuisine as well as for being the founding country of the Slow Food movement in the 1980s, started eating more u.s.-styled breakfast cereals in the twentieth century. Originally, Italians ate only two official meals during the day, like many other peoples. Indeed, in

Granola, the modern version of the breakfast cereal that started it all.

Roman times, the majority of the population ate wheat porridges throughout the day, made savoury with the addition of meat if it was available. Eventually, though, there came to be a designated morning 'breakfast' meal, *colazione*. (The Italian word *colazione* comes from the Latin *collationes*, meaning 'compilation' or 'collection', and the meal would be a compilation of available foods.) Prior to Italy's industrial revolution, most of the middle and working classes would have had some kind of porridge, often polenta, for their *colazione*, which was really just the first meal of the day and not necessarily what modern Europeans would now consider breakfast. Indeed, polenta became as synonymous with Italian gastronomy as grits were with the cuisine of the Southern United States, both iconic versions of porridge based on maize. By the twentieth century Italians had developed a 'typical' *colazione*, or breakfast, of coffee, milk, pastries and cold breakfast cereal. Italy provides one striking example of the introduction of cold breakfast cereal into a traditional cuisine, to some extent replacing a porridge or other customary sustaining food.[2]

Since their inception, breakfast cereal companies have aggressively advertised their foods. The same few corporations that started the breakfast cereal revolution in the 1900s have remained dominant into the 2020s. In the early years, cereal boxes were decorated with text and, later, images. Next, discount coupons and recipe books were inserted. Eventually, games and toy surprises were included in the cereal boxes. Advertisements were adapted over the years, evolving from appearing in print to being promoted on the radio, television and the Internet. Product sponsorship as well as the invention of recognizable mascots added interest and an element of nostalgia to cereal advertising.

Emotional appeals in advertising cross over into other areas of culture as well. Given the dominance of breakfast cereal, there is little wonder why it has been so well represented in arts and culture. All over the world, porridges and cold cereals appear in our stories, songs, festivals and visual arts. The ubiquity of breakfast cereal throughout culture shows its powerful role in human life.

The story of cereals' influence in culture and their evolution through scientific innovation continues into the twenty-first century, as companies and consumers work to imagine the future of breakfast cereal. However influential ready-to-eat cereals have grown, though, porridges are not going to be replaced on the global level any time soon. They are too deeply connected to human civilization itself. Since the earliest development of agriculture, humans have broken their night-time fast through a variety of what we now call 'breakfast foods'. Perhaps the least processed of the breakfast cereals, porridge remains a popular choice for breakfast around the world. The history of breakfast cereal shows that, ultimately, we return to the classics: traditional porridges as well as familiar cold cereal brands, such as Corn Flakes, Grape-Nuts, Cheerios, Quaker Oats and Weet-Bix. Simple, healthy and relatively cheap and comforting, breakfast cereals are perennially successful. Whether porridge or ready-to-eat, breakfast cereal is a global food.

I
Porridges around the World: Warm Breakfast Cereal

Pease Porridge hot,
Pease porridge cold,
Pease porridge in the pot,
Nine days old.
Traditional rhyme

Porridge is, unequivocally, the world's most common break-fast cereal, dating back almost as far as human civilization itself. Before the invention of cold breakfast cereals in the nineteenth century, cereals were almost entirely porridges, and to this day nearly every culture has some kind of iconic porridge dish in its cuisine, one based on a cereal grain such as maize, wheat or rice, among others. According to the *Oxford English Dictionary*, porridge was originally 'a thick soup' made of cereal grains, meat and vegetables. This kind of porridge was eaten for the majority of human history, before breakfast as a separate meal became standardized. A later definition, though, is closer to the current use of the word: a dish consisting of oat flakes, oatmeal or another meal (or flaked cereal) boiled in water or milk and often served for breakfast. As a breakfast cereal, porridge is commonly a grain cooked and served in water or milk, with optional accompaniments such as fruits, nuts or spices. Alternatively, porridge can be mixed with savoury spices and meats or fish. With this more advanced range of porridges, civilizations became possible.

In the tale of Jacob and Esau, the older brother, Esau, sells his birthright for 'bread and pottage of lentils', according to the King James Bible. 'Pottage' is a term for one of the earliest porridges, made possible after the development of the first ceramic cooking dishes, or pots, around 8,000 years ago. The invention of the ceramic pot allowed grains or pulses to be cooked in water like a stew, and this dish became known as a pottage. This form of a porridge was a breakthrough innovation, as it allowed people to eat a sustaining meal throughout the day that was softer than uncooked grains or legumes and therefore kinder to teeth. Thus Esau describes a form of savoury porridge in this passage, one comparable to a thick soup.

Similarly, in medieval times in Europe, a pease porridge, a dish like a pottage made from peas rather than grains, was a comforting meal popularized by a traditional children's rhyme, 'Pease Porridge Hot'. In fact, no less an icon of the modern age than Shakespeare jokes about porridge in his plays, using the current definition – that of a breakfast cereal – in *The Tempest*: 'He receives comfort like cold porridge' (II.1).

Just about the perfect food, porridges are easy, nutritious and cheap to prepare, and the primary grains used for porridge – wheat, oats, maize, rice, barley and rye – are together accountable for two-thirds of the total calories consumed by humans.[1] Porridge is thus a traditional element of the first meal of the day, what we now call 'breakfast', and has become a significant part of humanity's diet, specifically in the West.

However, breakfast as a separate meal is a relatively recent development, reliant on technological advances such as refrigeration and food preservation, since foods eaten soon

Jan Victors, *Esau and the Mess of Pottage*, 1653, oil on canvas.

after waking would have to be stored and kept safe over the course of the night. As the historian Andrew Dalby observes, prior to the Neolithic Revolution, people did not eat breakfast. Before the discovery of food-preservation methods, people had to eat their food relatively quickly after it was acquired, and logically, then, not first thing in the morning. Rather, the main meals occurred in the middle of the day – meals that, according to the *Oxford English Dictionary*, would become referred to as 'dinner'. This was most likely the primary significant meal of the day throughout early human civilizations, as well as for some human cultures into contemporary times.[2]

The etymology of the word 'breakfast', or 'breaking one's fast', comes originally from the Latin *disieiunare* or 'un-fast'. This term became the French *disdéjeuner*, which was condensed to *déjeuner* and eventually *petit déjeuner*. In another branch of the Latin root word, during the eleventh century, the French *disner* became the English term 'dinner'. Heather Arndt Anderson observes that the term 'breakfast' doesn't enter written English until the fifteenth century. As to the reason for the relatively late adoption of the term, she suggests, 'Either people did not eat it – and the startling dearth of written records would suggest this – or breakfast was obscured by the written accounts of the midday meals and evening feasts that were deemed more important.'[3] The breakfast meal is thus a relatively late development among human societies. A midday meal, though, involving a cereal grain with meats, vegetables and other additions – in other words, porridge – is truly ancient.

Since antiquity, three porridge grains – wheat, rice and maize – have been fundamental. At least 10,000 years ago, in the Fertile Crescent in the Middle East, people started cultivating the eight founder crops, including barley and two ancient forms of wheat, einkorn and emmer. Early agriculturists chose traits in these grains to make them more convenient for human use: heartiness and size. Improvements in agriculture led to bread wheat, most likely a hybrid of emmer wheat and an early goat grass, around 8,000 years ago. This became the common form of wheat. One of the most important elements of wheat was its ease of storage. Harvested wheat could be stored relatively simply for an extended period of time. Thus people did not have to consume their food immediately for fear of it going bad. While ground wheat does go bad quickly, if it is stored in seed form, and ground on an as-needed basis, the grain can be stored for much longer, and this provides food security. Wheat cultivation moved with human societies from the Middle East to the Mediterranean, as seen in this facsimile of an Egyptian crypt decoration depicting the harvesting of grains, specifically wheat and flax. Later, wheat domestication travelled to Europe as well as northern Asia, though it wasn't established firmly in Europe for cultivation until the nineteenth century. Currently, wheat is the second most cultivated grain in the world, following maize.[4]

Meanwhile, rice was first domesticated more than 10,000 years ago, around the Yangtze River Valley of China. From there, it migrated to the rest of Southeast Asia and eventually to Africa around 3,000 years ago. Currently, domesticated rice is the principal food for more than half of the world's population, most notably in Asia. From China and India, rice domestication spread throughout Asia, to Japan, Korea, the Philippines, Indonesia, Sri Lanka and beyond. Rice is labour intensive and requires a large amount of water to grow, which makes it suited to small-scale farming.

By 1000 CE, rice had helped China become the most productive economy in the world, largely based on an elaborate system of global trade built on a foundation of rice. China remained a dominant global power through the late eighteenth

Charles K. Wilkinson, *Sennedjem and Iineferti in the Fields of Iaru*, 1922, tempera on paper.

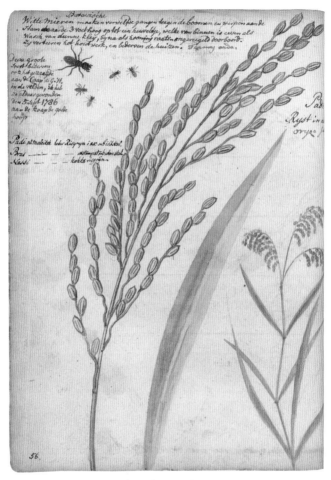

Jan Brandes, *Mieren en rijst*, 1786, drawing.

century and into the nineteenth century thanks largely to the production and distribution of rice. India and, later, Japan, among other nations, also established their economies and societies on the cultivation and consumption of rice. Today, as human populations increase, especially in the Asia-Pacific region, which is the most associated with rice consumption, rice will become even more in demand. In 2010 rice accounted for one-fifth of total human caloric intake.[5]

In Mesoamerica, what is today central Mexico through Central America, maize was cultivated around 10,000 years ago as well. Interestingly, maize developed in combination with human endeavour, and now there is a clear symbiotic relationship between the grain and humans. At some point, maize

Pierre François Legrand, *Maïs*, 1799–1801, ornament print.

grew beyond its ancestor, *teocinte*, into a sterile grass, a plant that needs human intervention in order to propagate.

Maize plants aren't able to disperse their own seeds; instead, they require humans to remove the tight husk from the kernels – the maize seeds – in order to consume and scatter them. Furthermore, the process of nixtamalization, cooking maize in an alkaline solution, is required to make it properly digestible for humans. Once these processes of agriculture and cultivation were established, though, maize travelled throughout the Americas and eventually to the rest of the world, becoming a significant cereal grain in West Africa and Europe, in particular.

Maize porridges were traditional in the Americas, as indigenous communities ate a porridge like the modern-day hominy as a staple. Another benefit of maize – as opposed to more fragile grains such as oats – is that it is relatively hearty, able to grow in a variety of environments. Maize is currently the most-produced grain in the world.[6]

Civilizations established foundational carbohydrate-rich foods, usually a cereal grain such as wheat, rice or maize, in as many as ten sites around the world independently. Each of those cereals developed into a regionally representative porridge. The importance of these sustaining porridges is often encoded in the language and culture of the particular regions associated with those grains. For example, wheat and barley were originally domesticated along the Fertile Crescent, where the earliest forms of writing – leading up to cuneiform – were being developed for the purpose of accounting for grains and other commodities.

Early clay tablets described planting methods, production organization and even recipes. An Egyptian limestone relief from the New Kingdom (1353–1336 BCE) gives a naturalistic representation of life-sized ears of barley. They are shown in motion, as if in a breeze. The fragment is assumed to be from the Amarna Period, during the reign of Akhenaten, and from a private tomb. During this time, both animals and plants were common themes in temples and in tombs. However, this example is noteworthy for its detail, emphasizing the prominence of grain in Egyptian culture. In another example, a model of a granary including scribes and other workers was found in the tomb of royal chief steward Meketre, who served during the eleventh and twelfth dynasties in Egypt during the reign of Amenemhat I. It deals with the preparation and accounting for grain. When considered that this model was buried with Meketre, it shows the importance of wheat and barley in the afterlife, as well as grain's connection to the concept of plenty.

Another region, ancient Rome, also used wheat as well as barley as its foundational porridge; the importance of these foundational grains is shown by the fact that the word 'cereal' is derived from the name of the Roman goddess of agriculture, Ceres.

Meanwhile, the primacy of rice as a staple is seen in the Japanese language as well. The word for 'rice' is embedded in the word for each of the daily meals: *gohan* means 'rice', as well

Ripe barley, *c.* 1353–1336 BCE, limestone, paint.

as 'meal' in general. 'Breakfast', 'lunch' and 'dinner' are known respectively as *asagohan*, *hirugohan* and *bangohan*.[7]

Traditional Japanese arts also reflect the importance of rice. In the print *Poem by Dainagon Tsunenobu (Minamoto no Tsunenobu, Katsura no Dainagon), from the series One Hundred Poems Explained by the Nurse* (1839), by the Japanese artist Katsushika Hokusai – whose 'Great Wave' print is among the most popular prints in the world – rice farmers are situated against a rural background. Everything about this print represents an idealized vision of traditional Japanese culture. Men carry their wares against a background of rice fields, with simple village houses and birds flying past. Women, meanwhile, are gathering water in the foreground. In addition, the image contains a poem: 'Now twilight darkens and the breeze rustles in the homeside rice fields, and murmuring sounds please my ears as the autumn gusts sweep past my hut thatched with ashi grass.' In both the poem and print, the rice fields are the setting of one's emotional ties – the land and what it grows to feed Japan's people are Hokusai's focus.

Katsushika Hokusai, *Poem by Dainagon Tsunenobu*, 1839, woodblock print.

Theodor de Bry, 'Food Preparation among Native Americans', 1591, engraving and text in letterpress.

Meanwhile, maize's dominance throughout the Americas can be seen in the legends of the Mesoamerican peoples, who worshipped maize deities and believed people were made from maize. Adrián Recinos's adaptation of the *Popol Vuh* describes the creation of humanity out of maize, or corn:

> After that they began to talk about the creation and the making of our first mother and father; of yellow corn and of white corn they made their flesh; of corn meal dough they made the arms and the legs of man. Only dough of corn meal went into the flesh of our first fathers, the four men, who were created.[8]

In the Old Testament creation story, the biblical deity creates humanity out of mud; in the K'iche' version, humanity begins from more sustaining elements, actual foodstuffs. The primacy of maize, or corn, in Latin American culture would never wane. Maize, as well as wheat and rice, have clear significance to civilizations throughout the world.

Wheat: Western Asia, Europe, North America

As a foundational crop, wheat spread from Asia to Europe, and from there to the Americas. The largest producers of wheat in the world are currently China, India, Russia and the United States. There is a wide variety of preparations of wheat porridges around the world. These include the popular 'cream of wheat' (Malt-O-Meal is a well-known brand) in the United States. Frumenty, a boiled wheat porridge, has been a traditional breakfast food in Europe since the Roman Empire. Northern India and Pakistan make a dish from cracked wheat called *dalia*, and southern India has a fried semolina porridge called *upma*. Meanwhile, Romania has a dish called *gris cu lapte*, a dessert-like porridge that can also be eaten for breakfast and is made with semolina boiled in milk with sugar and other additions. Hungary has a similar dish, *tejbegríz*, and Finland has *mannapuuro*. In Norway, *rømmegrøt* is a thick porridge of wheat flour cooked in sour cream and served with sugar and cinnamon, or cured meats and hard-boiled eggs. *Yarma* is a Turkish porridge made of wheat groats.

Rice: Asia, Africa, Europe, North America

Rice is considered one of the five key grains in China, one of its sites of origin. Congee is a rice porridge eaten in China and several other countries in Asia-Pacific; it is known by a variety of other names across the region: *kanji* in India, *kayu* in Japan and *juk* in Korea. It is prepared by cooking rice –

often glutinous rice – in water for an extended period of time, until it makes a thick gruel. It is often served as a savoury dish with meat, fish, vegetables, eggs, tofu and spices. Indeed, congee prepared with fish is a common breakfast food in various regions of China and throughout East Asia. What these regions have in common – and what separates their approach from most other preparations of breakfast porridges – is the commonality of congees as a vehicle for savoury flavours, rather than sweet. Congee is also considered a wholesome food to eat when someone isn't feeling well – a therapeutic comfort food. It remains popular enough worldwide that rice cookers often have a congee setting to allow for the cooking of rice to a desirably soft consistency.[9]

Other rice porridges around the world include *arroz caldo*, a rice porridge cooked with chicken broth and spices, and *champorado*, a sweet drink prepared with rice and chocolate, in the Philippines; *kheer*, an Indian sweet dish with rice boiled in milk; *frascarelli*, an Italian dish made of overcooked rice and white flour; *orez cu lapte*, a Romanian dessert-like food that can also be eaten for breakfast, which is made of rice boiled in milk with sugar and flavoured with spices, jam and cocoa; and *tejberizs*, a similar Hungarian dish. In North America, wild rice (a different rice cultivar than Asian rice) has been a significant food item for northern tribes. The Ojibwe and Potawatomi, for example, eat versions of steamed wild rice with maple syrup or cream for breakfast or as a pudding.

Maize: The Americas and Africa

In the Americas, maize has been the most important breakfast cereal grain since the early days of Mesoamerican civilization, and it quickly gained popularity worldwide following European contact. In fact, indigenous civilizations of the Americas established entire societies based on their relationship with maize. Amelia Simmons's *American Cookery* (1796) is the first instance of a Euro-American text describing a maize porridge, listing it under 'Indian Pudding'.

Maize porridges include grits and hasty pudding. Grits are the most popular form of maize porridge in the United States, especially in the South. They are made from boiled maize meal, or hominy, water or milk, as well as other flavours such as ham, cheese and butter (savoury) or sugar (sweet). These dishes can be eaten either savoury or sweet – when sweet, they are almost always consumed for breakfast. The word 'hominy' is thought to come from the Powhatan *rockahommie*.

Other preparations of maize found around the world include *atole*, a flavoured and drinkable gruel made of maize

Cooked hominy, maize treated with lime.

meal in Mexico. A form of *atole* with chocolate or other spices added is known as *champurrado*, a popular Mexican drink that can be consumed at breakfast or throughout the day.

Maize also spread to the African continent, where it was first seen as a novelty cereal grain. By the nineteenth century, though, it had become popular, and it has increased in production and consumption across the region ever since. The forms of maize porridge eaten across the African continent include *pap* in South Africa, *genfo* in Ethiopia, *nsima* in Zambia and Malawi, and *ugali* in Kenya, Tanzania, Uganda and elsewhere.[10]

Finally, the *kānga pirau* is a fermented maize porridge of the Maori culture that was a result of European colonialization; it has been fading in cultural popularity due to a widespread distaste for the strong odour produced during its preparation process.

Oats: Northern Europe

Oats are the most popular porridge grain throughout Europe, and European immigrants brought it with them to the Americas and Asia-Pacific. Oats are sensitive to summer heat, and are domesticated mostly in cooler regions, primarily in Europe – specifically in Russia, Scotland and Iceland – and North America. Ancient grains, oats have been found among the remains of 5,000-year-old European 'bog bodies', bodies that have been preserved naturally in peat bogs.[11]

Oatmeal, as oat porridge is termed in the United States, is one of the most popular preparations of this grain. Old-fashioned and instant oatmeal uses steamed and flattened oats. Steel-cut oatmeal uses the inner kernel of the grain chopped into pieces. Oatmeal is eaten regularly throughout Scotland,

The author's favourite breakfast cereal, oatmeal with apple, walnuts and cinnamon.

the UK, Ireland, Australia, New Zealand, North America and Scandinavia. It was considered a peasant food until the late nineteenth century, when the Quaker Oats Company popularized their packaged rolled oats in the United States. A twist on oatmeal is the English gruel (very thin – even drinkable), a traditional preparation. In Jane Austen's novels, for example, characters often request gruel. In *Emma* (1815), the character Mr Woodhouse comments, 'You and I will have a nice basin of gruel together.'[12] Elsewhere, such as in Russia, Poland and Ukraine, an oat dish called *owsianka* is made of hot milk, oats and sugar or butter. Stirabout is an Irish porridge made by stirring oats into boiling water or milk. *Terci de ovăz* and *zabkása* are traditional oat porridges in Romania and Hungary, respectively.

Barley: The Middle East, Africa, Europe

One of the oldest of the world's grains, barley was originally grown in the Fertile Crescent along with early breeds of wheat. Barley as well as wheat were the primary porridge foods of Mesopotamians as well as the Roman gladiators. Barley has also been eaten as a breakfast porridge historically and in modern times in Europe and North America. There is an English folk figure, John Barleycorn, named after the grain. Barley porridge, sometimes in a consistency comparable to gruel, is known as *sawiq* in the Middle East and northern Africa. In Norway, *byggrynsgrøt* is made from barley, with butter and milk or water. In Tibet, *tsampa* is a porridge made of toasted barley or wheat flour. A symbolic dish, the Dalai Lama himself has said he regularly eats it for breakfast, and it has come to represent Tibetan society more generally. *Ga'at* is an Ethiopian and Eritrean porridge often made from barley. In the Middle East, people consume a barley gruel called *talbina* made with honey or dates and milk.

Millet: Asia, Europe, Africa

Millet can be traced back 7,500 years to China – and it remains a significant porridge eaten as a breakfast food or snack throughout the Middle East, Russia and Germany. Millet is prepared in China as a popular dish called *chatang*. *Fondé* and *lakh* are two forms of millet porridge from Senegal usually prepared with sugar and dairy (either milk or butter). A dish called *uji* is eaten in Kenya, and a similar *ogi* is eaten in Nigeria – in either of these preparations, the grains are left to ferment for several days before eating. Meanwhile, the Ainu of Japan eat a *munchiro sayo*, a soup-like millet porridge. In Russia, millet is eaten either sweet or savoury, while in Germany, it is usually eaten sweet – with honey and apples. In India, *koozh* (or finger millet) porridge is associated with the Tamil festival of Mariamman.

Kasha: Asia, Europe, Africa

The Russian dish *kasha* is a porridge made of several grains mixed together, usually including buckwheat. *Kasha*'s significance to Russian people and culture is demonstrated by the fact that it has been made into a proverb, 'schi da kasha – pischa nasha' (or 'kasha and cabbage soup are our foods'). *Kasha* – using a variety of grains – is popular beyond Russia, in Eastern Europe and even in Africa. *Genfo*, while primarily made with maize, can also be made of mixed grains and legumes in Ethiopia. This medley of grains can be prepared savoury to be served at any time of the day, or with milk and sugar as more of a breakfast preparation.

Additional Porridges

There are a few other noteworthy global porridges, some of which aren't even grain based. Nigeria has a yam porridge called *asaro* in Yoruba. The Igbo people of Nigeria and Ghana have a traditional *Iri Ji* or 'New Yam' festival to celebrate the end of one harvest cycle and the beginning of the next in which an *asaro*-like yam porridge is prepared. Norway makes a potato porridge, *potetgrøt*, that is an almost-solid paste. In Ethiopia, *teff* – edible seeds of a bunch grass – is eaten as a traditional porridge, and a sorghum porridge, *mabela*, is a breakfast food in South Africa and Zimbabwe. In Canada, flax is often used in porridge, usually in combination with wheat and rye meal. *Ruispuuro* is a traditional Finnish breakfast porridge made with rye. Finally, Peru has a now-globally familiar quinoa porridge that can be eaten for breakfast or throughout the day.

Historically, porridge would be eaten throughout the day. In more recent years, and especially in the Western world, though, porridges have become more closely associated with breakfast. Breakfast porridges can be savoury or sweet, eaten with an almost-limitless variety of meat, fish, fruits, vegetables, nuts and spices. When a porridge is served sweet, though, it will almost certainly be served for breakfast. Alternatively, savoury porridges – a favourite style in Southeast Asia, parts of Africa and Latin America – can be served

Two of America's foundational cereals, corn and quinoa.

with beans, meat, fish and spices. Throughout all cultures, porridges, with a variety of grains as bases, have represented the most important meal of the day, at whatever hour it was consumed. By the time of the industrial revolutions across Europe and the United States, breakfast had become the morning meal. Breakfasts until the nineteenth century remained focused on warm porridge. However, a particular kind of food reform emerging in the United States during the nineteenth century would lead to an entirely different way to eat breakfast cereal: cold.

2
The Invention of Cold Breakfast Cereal

In the thirty-one years of his directorship, Dr. Kellogg had
transformed the San, as it was affectionately known, from
an Adventist boarding house specializing in Graham bread
and water cures to the 'Temple of Health' it had now become,
a place celebrated from coast to coast – and across the great wide
weltering Atlantic to London, Paris, Heidelberg and beyond.

T. C. Boyle, *The Road to Wellville* (1993)

Porridges are ubiquitous throughout human culture. Cold
breakfast cereals, on the other hand, date specifically to the
industrial period of the United States, the 1800s, and to one
man, Dr John Harvey Kellogg. The history of the development of ready-to-eat cereal, as opposed to porridge – as well
as the people involved in that story – is arguably more sensa-
tional than any nineteenth-century fiction could be. It has
been the subject of several books of history and fiction,
including T. C. Boyle's satire, *The Road to Wellville* (1993).
Named after one of C. W. Post's most influential promotional
materials, but focused on John Harvey Kellogg, Boyle's text
demonstrates the importance of the people who worked to
create a health movement, breakfast cereal and processed
food industry.

In the early nineteenth century, Americans were still eating large breakfasts and dinners – two main meals – daily. Labourers such as farmers would need the fuel to get through long and strenuous workdays. Their breakfasts were solid affairs, often including some kind of maize-based porridge, as well as meat or eggs. At the same time, wealthy Americans ate superior foods for their corresponding meals – for most of the nineteenth century, that included larger quantities of and better-quality meat.[1] This consumption of meat by the wealthy classes – along with other common dietary habits such as excessive alcohol consumption – resulted in health complaints such as dyspepsia, constipation and other gastro-intestinal disorders.

Due to these diet-related health issues, a food reform movement began in the mid-nineteenth century in the United States, with similar movements occurring across Europe at about the same time. Health reformers such as Sylvester

Woman stirring the porridge in a colonial-style room, *c.* 1914.

Graham, Ellen G. White, James Caleb Jackson, John Harvey and Will Keith (or W. K.) Kellogg, C. W. Post and Maximillian Bircher-Benner, among others, sought to bring wholegrains back into the nation's – and quickly the world's – diet. These reformers established sanatoriums, venues where client-patients would eat and live according to a 'scientific' method in order to improve their overall health, in large part through their diet. This movement gave rise to the foundational cold breakfast cereals – 'granula', the precursor to granola; Quaker Oats; and Corn Flakes and Grape-Nuts, the cereals from which all the rest have been adapted.[2]

The breakfast cereal movement was part of a larger history of reform in the mid- to late nineteenth century in North America, Europe and Australia. The most famous reform movements in the United States, for example, were abolition-ism (the fight against slavery), temperance (prohibition of alcohol) and the suffrage movement (women's right to vote). In the realm of the pseudosciences, moreover, this was also the time of mesmerism (akin to hypnotism), phrenology (studying the bumps in one's skull to determine personality traits) and even seances (contacting the dead). Diet reform was an import-ant part of the social and self-improvement fervour of the century.

The legacy of Sylvester Graham, the man who was, in large part, responsible for promoting vegetarianism in the United States and Europe, remains in the Graham cracker, his eponymous wholegrain wheat cracker which was developed in direct response to society's health concerns stemming from meat-heavy diets. One of the most famous diet reform-ers of the century, he had a series of 'Graham Houses' located throughout the United States, where devotees could live in vegetarian communities with like-minded Grahamites. His thoughts on diet, including vegetable-based diets, influenced

Kellogg's Corn Flakes, one of the first breakfast cereals and still one of the most popular across North America and Europe.

everyone else in this chapter, as each one applied Graham's dietary theories to the breakfast meal specifically.

The history of cold breakfast cereal dates back to 1863 and to one man: Dr James Caleb Jackson. A farmer-turned-reformer and abolitionist, Jackson had suffered from ill health throughout his early life. He found relief through the 'water cure', or hydrotherapy, a health movement in keeping with many of the other crusades of the time. The method behind hydrotherapy spas revolved around water – lots of water. Patients would take several baths and showers a day, drink excessive amounts of water (and often only water) through-out the day, all while eating only plain, healthy fare. In this way, it was believed, patients would repair their health. It worked for Jackson: he successfully regained his health through the water cure. After this, he was so enthusiastic about the cure that he quickly established his own spa in Dansville, New

York, spending the rest of his life working to heal his patient customers with hydrotherapy. Jackson included diet reform in his overall health philosophy at his Dansville spa, named 'Our Home on the Hillside'. He banned meat, coffee, tea, alcohol and tobacco from the premises, instead emphasizing the drinking of only water and non-stimulating, non-alcoholic beverages, as well as eating wholegrains, fruits and vegetables. It was against this setting that Jackson developed the first cold breakfast cereal.

Jackson started by baking a large flour wafer that he then broke into smaller, nugget-shaped biscuits. While it contained wholegrains – and was therefore a healthy food overall, one that would help with a variety of gastrointestinal ailments – Jackson's original breakfast cereal was excessively tough, requiring overnight soaking in water or milk in order to be palatable. It lacked the convenience people have since come to expect from breakfast cereal.[3] However, it was the first processed cold breakfast cereal, starting a revolution in food production and consumption. Though it was not commercially successful, Jackson's ideas about creating a healthy breakfast cereal to compete against the meat-heavy diet of the

Jackson's Sanitarium, from an 1890 publicity brochure.

United States would go on to influence other diet reformers such as Seventh-Day Adventist founder Ellen G. White, as well as her protégé, John Harvey Kellogg.

White was, by all accounts, a remarkable woman. She was one of the original founders of the Seventh-Day Adventist Church, a community that continues strong into the twenty-first century across the globe. As a member of one of the most prominent vegetarian communities of the nineteenth century, White visited Jackson's Dansville spa and was influenced by his dietary suggestions. Indeed, one of the Adventist communities White helped to form, in Loma Linda, California, has earned a place along with Nicoya, Costa Rica; Okinawa, Japan; Sardinia, Italy; and Icaria, Greece, as one of the world's 'Blue Zone' regions, areas known for the health and longevity of their residents. Before she moved to California, though, she helped establish the Sanitarium in Battle Creek, Michigan, based in part on the ideas she learned from Jackson's Dansville spa. Moreover, she brought the young doctor, John Harvey Kellogg, to help her run the Sanitarium.

Kellogg was a Michigan native raised as a Seventh-Day Adventist. He and his brother W. K. Kellogg were two of seventeen siblings and half-siblings. In John Harvey's youth, White took an interest in his education, helping him by funding his schooling at the University of Michigan, New York University and Bellevue Hospital, where he studied to become a medical doctor. Shortly after his graduation, he joined the Battle Creek Medical Surgical Sanitarium – renamed the Battle Creek Sanitarium – in 1876, working directly under the Whites. He then visited 'Our Home on the Hillside' at Dansville, in 1878, with White. There, they sought to learn from Jackson's ideas of diet reform for health and wellness, to bring those ideas back to the Sanitarium. Kellogg was a practising physician, and his health-food interests were rooted in the cutting-edge science of the late nineteenth century. His nutrition advocacy, moreover, was fashionable during the time and has had a lasting impact.

Kellogg is, without a doubt, the most important single figure in the history of cold breakfast cereal. Part of his diet reform plan was to aid his patients' digestion by producing already partially processed – he called them 'pre-digested' – foods that would be easier for delicate systems to manage. Kellogg's processed breakfast foods were part of his larger 'biologic living' philosophy at the Sanitarium, informally referred to as 'the San'. He connected his dietary concerns with his understanding of the germ theory of disease, focusing largely on the bacteria of the stomach and intestines; he was an early advocate for research on what we now call the microbiome. A healthy diet, he realized, was the key to overall health, and he continually practised and developed new recipes through his test kitchen at the Sanitarium. As a skilled physician and surgeon, Kellogg also worked throughout his career to avoid the need for surgery, when possible, through dietary adjustments.[4]

Though a respected doctor and nutritionist throughout his life, Kellogg's history has become more complicated over time. Kellogg eventually left White's community under difficult circumstances, but despite being excommunicated from the church, he remained in charge of the Battle Creek Sanitarium, while the Whites and their followers left Michigan for California. Kellogg and his wife, Ella Eaton Kellogg, who was also a health reformer and writer, never had biological children, instead fostering 42 children. He believed in eugenics, the idea of scientific breeding that is racist in its fundamental assumptions. Indeed, Kellogg believed in the separation of races, and in 1906 he co-founded the Race Betterment Foundation. While he was a challenging figure, his dietary inventions – specifically his breakfast cereals – remain culturally significant to this day.

John Harvey and Ella Eaton Kellogg continually practised and developed new recipes through the Sanitarium's experimental kitchen, with Ella having the role of directly supervising the working of the kitchen. Perhaps unsurprisingly, Ella's work in the development of modern breakfast cereal is often overlooked. In the Sanitarium's test kitchen, the Kelloggs – including W. K. – made a number of healthy breakfast food recipes, some of which were published in Ella's book, *Science in the Kitchen* (1892). One of their first recipes was a version of granula, served for breakfast at the Sanitarium starting in 1878. The Kellogg recipe closely followed Jackson's original, whether by accident or design, with one subtle difference: it added cornmeal and oatmeal to the coarse wheat flour of the original. The Kellogg granula was also slowly

John Harvey Kellogg giving a presentation at the Battle Creek Sanitarium, *c.* 1930s.

Cover image of E. E. Kellogg, *Science in the Kitchen* (1893 edn).

baked and ground into bits. While this breakfast cereal was an improvement on earlier recipes at the Sanitarium, it was strikingly similar to Jackson's original granula. Indeed, the recipe was close enough – and bore the same name – for Jackson to threaten litigation, and so began John Harvey's long history of lawsuits. To avoid being sued by Jackson for infringement of copyright, the Kelloggs changed the name of their version to granola. This was still a hard, relatively bland cereal that was treated as a health food for patients at the Sanitarium, rather than in the wider market, as it was too plain and far too expensive to market successfully to the overall population.

President Taft visiting Battle Creek, Michigan, with John Harvey Kellogg, Will Keith Kellogg and C. W. Post in attendance.

Eventually, the Kelloggs developed a better flaked cereal, which would become the iconic Kellogg's Corn Flakes, and an industry was born. John Harvey patented his flakes – at the time made from wheat – in 1894 as 'Flaked Cereals and Process of Preparing Same'. In this patent, Kellogg described his process of cooking grain, rolling it out and then baking it again: 'The finished product thus consists of extremely thin flakes, in which the bran (or the cellulose portion thereof) is disintegrated and which have been thoroughly cooked and prepared for the digestive processes by digestion, thorough cooking, steaming, and roasting.'[5] Kellogg took the time to make sure that his unique process was protected by u.s. patent laws, but he failed to mention other aspects of his invention outside of his direct influence. He did not cite any other food products within his patent, nor did he mention the manufacturer of his equipment. In other words, he left the field open for competitors, who quickly took advantage of this opportunity during the breakfast cereal boom.

This early patent gives a direct look into Kellogg's philosophy about the importance of his cereal products. His patent, much like the food invention it describes, was the first of its kind and set the basis for later, similar cereal food products, as well as the concern over intellectual property that has been involved in the patenting process of cold breakfast cereals ever since. Kellogg would unsuccessfully sue Henry Perky when the latter began production of what would become Shredded Wheat in 1895. However, it was decided that the patent in question was too unspecific to be limiting of other cereal developments. Overall, while Kellogg's patent does not contain many specifics – it generalizes 'flakes' rather than specifying wheat flakes, for example – it makes up for this with the fact that it spawned an entire breakfast cereal industry.[6]

The theme of lawsuits is particularly relevant in Kellogg's relationship with his brother, W. K. Kellogg. In 1879 W. K. joined his brother John Harvey at the Sanitarium, as his assistant. During this time, John Harvey used to give frequent tours of his test kitchen to visitors and patients, allowing detailed examination of his recipes and techniques. During his own health-based visit to the Sanitarium, C. W. Post took advantage of this. Post stole the Kellogg family's idea of flaked cereal and developed the Post Cereal Company from it. Discovering this, the younger Kellogg brother wanted to fight back by creating a breakfast cereal company to compete with Post. Together with John Harvey, he developed the Sanitas Food Company in 1897.

One of the brothers' fights, however, was over the quantities of added sugar in their cereals. John Harvey adamantly refused to add significant additional sugar to his breakfast cereals. However, W. K. rightly observed that without the enhancement, their cereals were overly bland and would sell poorly. Eventually, the relationship between the brothers became overly strained and they realized they could no longer work together, and W. K. left the Sanitarium to form what would become known as the Kellogg Cereal Company, specializing in breakfast cereals with the addition of sugar (though not in the amounts known since the mid-twentieth century), following the example of C. W. Post. In fact, W. K.'s frustration with Post's capitalizing on the Kellogg invention caused him to market his cereal with a 'Kellogg's' signature on each box as a sign of its authenticity, implying Post's inauthenticity as his cereal boxes lacked such a signature. John Harvey never approved of the materialism of W. K.'s business-mindedness, and they remained fundamentally estranged for the rest of their lives, sometimes even to the point of fighting each other in court. Interestingly, though they fought throughout most of their adult lives, they must have done something right: both Kellogg brothers lived into their nineties.

Will Keith Kellogg standing next to one of his beloved horses and with his daughter Beth and grandchildren, view from Kellogg mansion, late 1920s, postcard.

Furthermore, as an antagonist, W. K. makes for a disappointing figure, being more civic-minded than the average successful business tycoon. He helped arrange payment for the treatment of poor patients while he worked at the Sanitarium; he created a series of employee benefits at his early breakfast cereal factory that were ahead of their time, such as playgrounds for the children of employees as well as parks; he put nutrition labels on his products before the rest of the industry; and in 1930, in the midst of the Great Depression in the USA, he created the W. K. Kellogg Foundation – a charitable institution that remains active in Battle Creek to this day. Indeed, his $66 million donation, which helped to establish the foundation, would equate to more than $1 billion in the twenty-first century. One could say that W. K. fulfilled his pledge: 'I'll invest my money in people.'

John Harvey Kellogg's antagonist C. W. Post was a patient at the Sanitarium in 1891, having suffered from digestive issues throughout most of his adult life. He was impressed by the revival of his health and the overall health benefits that came with adhering to Kellogg's diet, and he became fascinated by the chemistry involved. An ambitious, and now relatively healthy, man, Post took over the running of La Vita Inn in Battle Creek, Michigan, a neighbour and competitor to the Sanitarium. He wanted to go beyond Kellogg's level of success, though. In addition to developing a coffee substitute called Postum – which is still available in health-food stores and restaurants in the USA – Post patented his own cereal, Grape-Nuts, in 1897. To make his iconic breakfast cereal, Post took a sheet of whole-wheat batter and broke it into bits that were then ground into the nugget-sized pieces recognizable to this day. This became one of the most popular cereals in history. Made with neither grapes nor nuts, Grape-Nuts was named for the cereal's use of maltose sugar, which Post

C. W. Post,
c. 1914.

called 'grape sugar', and for the nutty flavour the nuggets achieved through the toasting process.

The success of Grape-Nuts allowed Post to establish The Postum Cereal Company, forerunner of Post Cereal Company, as a major entity – directly in competition with its neighbour, Sanitas and, later, Kellogg Cereal Company. A classic rags-to-riches story, Post went from invalid to millionaire in six years. As opposed to the Kelloggs, though, Post's good health did not last. He was operated on by the famous doctors William and Charles Mayo at their Minnesota clinic for a case of appendicitis in 1914. Though the Mayo brothers called their operation a success, Post remained in great pain, and within months, he had committed suicide at the age of 59.[7]

The epicentre of much of this breakfast cereal drama, Battle Creek, has an iconic story, as well. A veritable boom town of 30,000 residents, it was, at the turn of the century, comparable to any mining town at its peak. But Battle Creek's 'klondike' was in breakfast cereal. Some of the nicknames given to the city around this time were 'The World's Cereal Bowl', 'Cereal City', 'Foodtown' and 'Cornflake Capital of the World'.[8] Battle Creek, named after a battle between Europeans and the indigenous Potawatomi in the early 1800s, will forever be remembered for the breakfast cereal boom, and as the current site of the global headquarters for Kellogg Cereal Company, as well as the W. K. Kellogg Foundation. While the cereal boom has, to a large extent, moved beyond Battle Creek, the stories – and some of the corporate offices – remain.

The Battle Creek breakfast cereal boom quickly moved beyond the United States. A Swiss doctor and nutritionist, Maximilian Oskar Bircher-Benner, opened a Zurich sanatorium called 'Vital Force' in 1897, around the same time that John Harvey Kellogg was working on healthful pre-digested breakfast cereals at his Sanitarium. At his Zurich spa, Bircher-Benner served a raw food diet to help patients heal from a variety of health concerns, focusing on those connected to digestive health. Bircher-Benner came to be involved in food reform in a familiar way, following his own bout of jaundice that he believed was cured by his consumption of raw foods – specifically apples. Going beyond vegetarianism, beyond the strict diets of Jackson and Kellogg, Bircher-Benner advocated a raw food diet as the most nutritious way to eat. His interest in diet, in raw food and in its health benefits to patients at Vital Force resulted in the development of his own breakfast cereal, *Birchermüesli*, more commonly known as müesli or muesli, around 1906.

Bircher-Benner's original recipe included uncooked rolled oats, fruit and nuts, and it is in many ways comparable to modern-day granola, though with uncooked oats. The dish was

The simple ingredients used to make Maximilian Bircher-Benner's *Birchermüesli*.

inspired by one his family had tried while hiking in the Swiss Alps. As opposed to the Kellogg example, Bircher-Benner argued against processing or baking his breakfast foods. He wanted his patients to do the work of digestion themselves. In addition, and unlike modern-day breakfast cereals, Bircher-Benner fed his patients müesli throughout the day – often at every meal. His breakfast cereal innovation, unlike that of Kellogg or Post, was easy to make at home with a few simple ingredients. His invention did not start out as a specific packaged breakfast food that could be be sold in stores. Perhaps this is why Bircher-Benner's name is not now associated with a multinational breakfast cereal corporation.[9]

3
Breakfast Cereal since the Nineteenth Century around the World

Ifemelu told her about the vertigo she had felt the first time
she went to the supermarket; in the cereal aisle, she had wanted
to get corn flakes, which she was used to eating back home,
but suddenly confronted by a hundred different cereal boxes,
in a swirl of colors and images, she had fought dizziness.
She told this story because she thought it was funny;
it appealed harmlessly to the American ego.
Chimamanda Ngozi Adichie, *Americanah* (2013)

As u.s. cargo ships travelled to markets around the world in
the early twentieth century, they visited ports in various countries and territories, including South Africa, Hong Kong and
Cairo. As they did, they brought ready-to-eat breakfast cereals
to these markets along with their other freight.[1] The rapid
globalization of what had started out as a u.s. foodstuff
shows how interconnected the world already was at the time
of the breakfast cereal boom. By the 1950s, in fact, Canadians
and Australians were eating more breakfast cereal per capita
than u.s. families.[2] Since that time, ready-to-eat cereals have
competed with traditional porridges for market shares
throughout the world. The profusion of these cereals appears

in Nigerian American author Chimamanda Ngozi Adichie's *Americanah* (2013). Her character Ifemelu develops a sense of vertigo when confronting perhaps the most iconic aisle in any u.s. grocery store: the breakfast cereal aisle. As opposed to a foundational *fufu* or *sadza*, traditional Nigerian porridges, or even a generic box of cornflakes, the Western breakfast cereals in this scene do not leave the character feeling satisfied and nourished, but rather unsteady.

While Asia, Africa and South America have historically had less interest in cold breakfast cereals, remaining true to their savoury traditional porridges, that has been changing since the second half of the twentieth century for a number of reasons. Ready-to-eat cereals were deemed healthy foods that were fast and easy to prepare – easy enough for an unsupervised child to do. They were convenient breakfast foods for urban workers to eat before their daily shifts, as well.

Puffed Rice booth at the Louisiana Purchase Exposition, 1904.

The rise of supermarkets made breakfast cereals available to greater numbers of people across the world at a low cost compared to other breakfast food options. Finally, expanding breakfast cereal companies such as Kellogg, Post and Quaker Oats spent vast amounts of money and ingenuity promoting their cereals.

In addition to their strategies to expand to larger markets worldwide, competition has also been a motivating factor for breakfast cereal companies almost since the beginning. This competition drove companies to invent ever-more-elaborate innovations in their cereals. Alexander P. Anderson's puffing gun, developed in 1902, is one such example. This machine would 'pop' a cereal to make it into a puff, an 'O' or other forms or shapes that are now as common as the original breakfast cereal flakes or nuggets. The moisture in the starch of a cereal grain, when pressurized and heated to a very high temperature (around 260° Celsius or 500° Fahrenheit), turned to steam quickly, expanding the grains of whatever cereal was being run through the gun. This resulted in a cereal 'puff'. Anderson presented his discovery at the 1904 Louisiana Purchase Exposition world's fair in St Louis, Missouri, puffing rice to an audience that included, over the course of the fair, the likes of Thomas Edison and Alexander Graham Bell. The first puffed maize (or corn) cereal was Kix, followed by Cheerioats, the precursor to Cheerios, as well as Corn Pops and Lucky Charms, among others. While the puffing gun was replaced in the 1940s for more efficient extruding machines, all non-flake or nugget forms of breakfast cereal use some version of the extrusion process first established in 1902.

The fact that breakfast cereal is a processed food also allowed it to become a more healthful, or functional, food than it had been at the various late nineteenth-century health spas where it was part of a healthy diet. During the first half

Corn Pops, the new cereal shapes.

of the twentieth century, the U.S. Food and Drug Administration sought to remedy debilitating juvenile diseases such as rickets (caused by vitamin D deficiency) and pellagra (caused by nicotinic acid deficiency, often associated with over-dependence on maize) that were affecting families throughout the world. Breakfast cereal companies responded, fortifying their foods with minerals and vitamins including iron, ribo-flavin, thiamin (also known as vitamin B1) and niacin, as well as calcium and vitamin D. The word 'vitamin', a derivative of the term 'vitamine', was coined by the Polish scientist Casimir Funk in 1912. He developed his vitamine shortly after the Japanese scientist Umetaro Suzuki discovered a way to cure patients of beriberi in 1910 by using a combination of micro-nutrients he named acerbic acid and which we now call vita-min B1 or thiamin. Though Suzuki found the nutrient before Funk, and therefore discovered vitamins first, his work had not been translated into German by 1912 and was therefore

Umetaro Suzuki, the original developer of what would become known as vitamins.

inaccessible to Funk, who ultimately received the credit for naming the 'vitamine'. Societies around the world had already made the connection between food and health, but Suzuki and Funk established this particular element of health in diet. Breakfast cereal, with these important vitamins and minerals added to it, has been credited for removing various diseases such as pellagra from the United States, Europe and other cereal-consuming regions. Since the 1930s and 1940s, breakfast cereals – usually consumed with protein-rich milk – have indeed been part of a healthy breakfast. Thus the health concerns originally addressed by John Harvey Kellogg continued into the twentieth century, but, in some ways, methods for

One of the author's favourite breakfast cereal treats, Kellogg's Frosted Mini-Wheats.

addressing them were improved upon by the corporations of which Kellogg's was only one.[3]

Vitamins and minerals were not the only supplemental ingredients being added to these breakfast cereals, though. In 1939 Jim Rex developed the technology to add a coating of syrup and honey to puffed cereals, before baking them at high temperatures to thoroughly and evenly distribute the sweet coating. Rex's pre-frosted breakfast cereal was named Ranger Joe Popped Wheat Honnies, in honour of the popular Lone Ranger character. At the time, the pre-sweetened cereal was considered to be a healthy alternative to the tendency of consumers, specifically children, to add unknown quantities of sugar to their breakfast cereal. However, Rex was not the savvy businessman that either C. W. Post or W. K. Kellogg was, and production issues were compounded by his overall lack of business know-how. Furthermore, the cereal's sugary coating tended to melt and resolidify too easily, turning it into unappetizing globs. His Ranger Joe Breakfast Food Company closed in less than a year. The concept of a 'frosted' cereal, though, was quickly picked up by Post, Kellogg and the rest of the breakfast cereal industry. Within the next decade, Post had developed Sugar Crisp, the company's own version of a puffed pre-sweetened cereal, and by 1952, Kellogg had added Frosted Flakes to its roster, and others followed, including Frosted Mini-Wheats in 1969.[4]

Meanwhile, the health reform movements that spawned the original ready-to-eat breakfast cereals also created other versions of these staples around the world. In Australia, New Zealand and South Africa, for example, Weet-Bix became as iconic as Grape-Nuts or Corn Flakes were in the United States. This wholegrain cereal consisted of wheat formed into rect-angular biscuits, usually eaten cold with milk. In the early twentieth century, the Seventh-Day Adventists, led by Ellen G. White, developed the Sanitarium Health Food Company from their base of operations in Australia. The company pur-chased the Australian rights for Weet-Bix in 1928, according

Weet-Bix,
Australia's
favourite
breakfast
cereal.

Weet-Bix advertisement, 1948.

to the company website, after which the cereal spread to New Zealand and South Africa, and then to Britain in 1932, where its name was changed to Weetabix. The Weet-Bix website proclaims 'Aussie kids are Weet-Bix kids'. In New Zealand, moreover, the Weet-Bix box makes the claim of being the country's 'No. 1 Breakfast Cereal'. All versions of this iconic breakfast cereal have remained popular in their respective countries.[5]

The success of ready-to-eat breakfast cereals around the world came largely from their convenience. As more women entered the workforce – and as a greater number of households included multiple working adults – parents sought

Modern-day granola, which began as a return to healthy breakfast cereal in the 1960s.

convenient and healthy ways to feed their families a meal to start the day. The unique appeal of breakfast cereals further stems from their ease of use. Even small children can operate the boxes, milk and dishes with little adult supervision – something unimaginable in the case of preparing hot porridges that involve boiling water and operating hot stoves. This convenience has proved crucial for busy parents looking after their families in the morning.

By the 1960s, though, health-conscious parents craved convenient as well as wholesome foods for their family breakfasts. Layton Gentry (nicknamed Johnny Granola-Seed) redesigned granola at this time, offering a less sugary alternative to the breakfast cereals that were, by now, ubiquitous in the cereal aisles of grocery stores in North America, Europe and increasingly the rest of the world. He based his formula on Kellogg's original patented version of granola from the nineteenth century, but he changed it by adding nuts and seeds to his 'Crunchy Granola'; he also added a sweetener such as syrup or brown sugar, though in lower amounts than his breakfast cereal competition. It was a counter-culture response to sugary breakfast cereals.

Pet Incorporated, a St Louis, Missouri, company, developed the first packaged granola brand, Hartland Natural Cereal, in 1972. It was marketed as a nostalgic cereal, with design choices including sepia tones on their cereal boxes and advertising, reminding consumers of an earlier time when cereals were health foods. Crunchy granola became wildly popular among consumers, and breakfast cereal companies quickly developed their own versions of Gentry's recipe. Soon more or less every breakfast cereal company had a granola as part of its range. Today granola is fully mainstream, with countless flavour iterations and scales of production. Small-batch, artisanal granolas were particularly popular in the 2010s.

Interestingly, granola, like müesli, is also perhaps one of the most easily adapted breakfast cereals for making at home. It is perhaps for this reason that – like Bircher-Benner and his müesli – the name Gentry is not as well known as either Kellogg or Post.[6]

By the 1970s, breakfast cereal companies were being pressured to make less sugary versions of all of their cereals. Most responded, advertising the addition of more wholegrains, bran or nuts to their products, or options for consumers with dietary restrictions, such as gluten-free. Breakfast cereal companies also rebranded their cereals, changing the names of Sugar Smacks to Honey Smacks and Sugar Pops to Corn Pops, for example. However, while the word 'sugar' was removed from these titles, the sugar content was often not actually altered in these and many other cases.[7]

An example of the modern tension between pre-sweetened, ready-to-eat breakfast cereal and more healthful porridges can be seen in the first two books of J. K. Rowling's Harry Potter series. (Rowling has become a controversial figure in the 2020s. Nevertheless, her Harry Potter series has been profoundly influential for generations of readers.) In *Harry Potter and the Philosopher's Stone* (1997; *Sorcerer's Stone* in the U.S. publication), breakfast cereal is associated with the muggle world, the non-magical parallel world that is decidedly less interesting than the magical world of the wizarding school Hogwarts. Early in the novel, Harry's spoiled infant cousin, Dudley, is seen 'having a tantrum and throwing his cereal at the walls'. Later, Harry's relatives, on the run from his magical destiny, eat breakfast at a remote hotel. 'They ate stale cornflakes and cold tinned tomatoes for breakfast the next day.'[8] Rowling is careful to make the cornflakes stale, as well as generic. They are not capitalized; rather, they are shown to be the default of boring boxed cereals. This is contrasted with her descriptions of the delicious breakfasts and other meals served at Hogwarts. In *Harry Potter and the Chamber of Secrets* (1998), for example, she writes, 'The four long House tables were laden with tureens of porridge, plates of kippers, mountains of toast, and dishes of eggs and bacon, beneath the enchanted ceiling.'[9] While Rowling famously emphasizes traditional British cuisine in her stories, that is not her sole intent in this scene. Rather, this is a classic example of fantasy fulfilment for a young boy who has not had enough to eat throughout his childhood. The breakfast foods – and here porridge is emphasized, not ready-to-eat breakfast cereals – are comforting and plentiful. Harry and his friends will be well nourished at their school of magic.

Breakfast cereal companies are working as diligently as ever to cater for an ever-expanding global population, fictional or otherwise. The major breakfast cereal corporations of the twentieth century have remained the biggest in the early twenty-first century. The largest five companies are Kellogg, General Mills, Cereal Partners Worldwide (a conglomeration of General Mills and Nestlé outside the United States and

'The Largest Manufacturers of Ready-to-Eat Cereal Foods in the World', postcard.

Packing room, Kellogg Company, Battle Creek, Michigan, postcard.

Canada), PepsiCo (current parent company of Quaker Oats) and Post Consumer Brands. In 2021, Kellogg was perhaps the most influential breakfast cereal company, one of the foundational companies and still the largest. In the 1980s, Kellogg aggressively developed cereals to market towards countries outside of North America and Europe, creating Just Right for the Australian market and Genmai Flakes for Japan. The Kellogg company website notes that its cereals are sold in more than 180 countries around the world. In fact, the company's largest manufacturing plant isn't even in the United States, but at Trafford Park in the UK. Some of Kellogg's popular cereals in North America include All-Bran, Coco Pops, Froot Loops, Frosted Flakes, Frosted Mini-Wheats, Rice Krispies and, in Canada, Vector, in addition to the cereal that started it all, Corn Flakes. Worldwide, Kellogg's popular brands of cereal include Kringelz in Germany, Chocos in India, Strawberry Pops in South Africa and Choco Krispis in Latin America.

While Kellogg has the largest share of the global breakfast cereal trade, General Mills and the Swiss-originated company

Granola advertisement, 1893.

Nestlé also have significant shares of the competitive market. The two companies formed Cereal Partners Worldwide in 1990, a move that allowed General Mills to sell its cereals under the globally recognized Nestlé brand, while remaining distinct companies. Like its multinational peers, Cereal Partners Worldwide sells breakfast cereals in more than 180 countries. General Mills began as Minneapolis Milling Company in 1856, and then merged with other mills to form the company General Mills in 1928. Since then, its influence has grown to the point where its cereal brands are nearly as recognizable as those of either Kellogg or Post. Its noteworthy cereals are the perennially popular 'Monster Cereals' such as Count Chocula and Franken Berry, as well as Cocoa Puffs, Lucky Charms, Wheaties and, especially, Cheerios.

Nor did Nestlé begin as a breakfast cereal company, but rather in 1866 as the Anglo-Swiss Condensed Milk Company. Its interests quickly expanded to cereal, though – especially as cereal complemented its original product of milk. Nestlé has a bigger presence on the global stage than General Mills. Some of its noteworthy global brands are Golden Morn in

Nigeria, Cerevita in Zimbabwe and Ghana, Nescau Cereal in Brazil and Shreddies in the UK and Ireland. Of the major multinational breakfast cereal companies, Nestlé is the lone example of one that did not originate in the United States.

The American Cereal Company, originally established in 1877 and known more familiarly as Quaker Oats Company, was acquired by PepsiCo in 2001. Well before this merger, though, in 1893, the company moved a marketing division to London, increasing its presence in the UK and Europe in the first half of the twentieth century.[10] The company's most popular cereal globally is Quaker Oats. In addition to its Quaker oatmeal brand, and the early technological marvel of Quaker Puffed Rice, it also sells Cap'n Crunch and Life cereals, as well as another porridge, Quaker Grits.

Rounding out the top global breakfast cereal companies of the early twenty-first century is another of the originals, Post, currently named Post Consumer Brands. Post produces its iconic Grape-Nuts, Cocoa and Fruity Pebbles, Honey

Cereal aisle, Oman. Note the Arabic letters on the Temmy's Choco Pops and Fruit Rings cereals.

Bunches of Oats, Raisin Bran and Shredded Wheat, among other cold cereals – and the porridge Malt-O-Meal for the North American market. The company also produces the cereal Shreddies throughout the Commonwealth and Germany (except for in the UK and Ireland, where it's produced by Cereal Partners Worldwide), Oreo O's in South Korea and 100% Bran in Canada. In addition, though the Post brand remains primarily based in North America – as opposed to the more globally recognized brands like Nestlé – after a dizzying series of mergers and acquisitions, Post also currently produces Weetabix and Weetos in the UK. These breakfast cereal corporations have become truly global in scale, but in many ways, they are similar to the foundational companies that in the late nineteenth century began the cold breakfast cereal industry.

Truly, breakfast cereals have always been global, both porridges and cold breakfast cereals, and this has only intensified into the twenty-first century. Food shops from North America to East Asia and the Middle East have aisles stocked with breakfast cereals that are promoted by multinational corporations, as well as regionally specific brands with their own area names, themes, mascots and flavour combinations. An article in the *Washington Post* in March 2015 named the most popular breakfast cereals, covering the prevalence of ready-to-eat cereals across the globe. In the United States, for example, Cheerios – especially Honey Nut Cheerios – Frosted Flakes, Cinnamon Toast Crunch and Lucky Charms remain popular in the twenty-first century. On the other hand, Wheaties, Trix and Corn Pops have started falling behind in popularity. Examples of popular cold breakfast cereals worldwide include Weetabix in Britain, Weet-Bix and Uncle Toby's Shredded Wheat in Australia, Post's Oreo O's in South Korea, Nestlé's Golden Morn in Nigeria and Temmy's Fruit Rings in

Oman. By the late 2010s, grocery stores with breakfast cereal aisles were ubiquitous throughout the world. Anyone could go to the cereal aisle of a shop in Muscat, Oman, for example, and see many of the same breakfast cereals enjoyed in North America and Europe, such as Kellogg's Rice Krispies and Quaker Oats' Cap'n Crunch as well as regional Temmy's Choco Pops and Fruit Rings cereals.

American Cereal Co. advertisement, *c.* 1880.

4
Marketing and Breakfast Cereal

Please, sir . . . I want some more.

Charles Dickens, *Oliver Twist* (1837)

Cold breakfast cereals started as health foods, but they were, from the beginning, also some of the most heavily marketed foods in history – cereal corporations have worked diligently to keep the cereal-eating public wanting more. The popularity of these cereals – as well as their fundamental connection to marketing – is shown in a satirical story written by the British author H. H. Munro, under the pen name Saki, in 1911. The story, 'Filboid Studge: The Story of a Mouse that Helped', describes a fictional breakfast cereal, Pipenta, that is successfully rebranded as Filboid Studge. The cereal is advertised not through positive associations (healthy babies and the like), but rather through the customers' fear of Hell and Lost Souls. The advertisement in the story notes regretfully, 'They cannot buy it now.' Meanwhile, Saki observes that his character Mark Spayley 'had grasped the fact that people will do things from a sense of duty which they would never attempt as a pleasure . . . And so it was with the new breakfast food.' The story ends with the character worried that the supremacy of his cereal, Filboid Studge, 'would be challenged as soon as a yet

A child eats Quaker Puffed Rice, *c.* 1918.

more unpalatable food should be put on the market'.[1] In this humorous depiction of an exaggerated story of breakfast cereal and marketing, 'Filboid Studge' shows that breakfast cereal had, by the early twentieth century, truly arrived. The cold cereals of the kind developed by John Harvey Kellogg, C. W. Post and Maximilian Bircher-Benner were by then being mocked as morally unimpeachable and 'unpalatable'.

C. W. Post, creator of Grape-Nuts cereal, was the 'grandfather of American advertising'.[2] His marketing efforts were largely what made breakfast cereal a staple for the morning meal across the United States, Europe and eventually the world. Post claimed any number of health benefits from consuming his products, from the coffee substitute Postum to breakfast cereals Elijah's Manna – later known as Post Toasties – and Grape-Nuts. Post took advantage of all opportunities to sell his products, including making claims about the food on the packaging itself. One of the earliest boxes of Grape-Nuts reads, 'Fully cooked, Pre-digested, Breakfast food/ Grape-Nuts/ A food for the brain and nerve centers'. Post also created print advertisements that appeared regularly in newspapers across the country, sometimes using a medical theme, guilt or a folksy narrative style. A magazine from the turn of the century, *Success*, named C. W. Post its advertiser of note for the year 1903. In almost every month throughout that year, the magazine featured an advertisement from the Post Company for Grape-Nuts Cereal. In the early years of his company, Post worried about the expenses of advertising, observing in a letter to his brother that he spent $981.78 on advertising alone in 1896. However, he persevered with his large marketing budget, eventually finding that his instincts had been correct. In 1897 he sold close to $262,280 worth of Post goods, or the equivalent of nearly $8.2 million in 2020 u.s. dollars, according to Official Data Foundation. This is even before his 1898 patenting of the iconic Grape-Nuts brand.

While Post was an early, unabashed promoter of pack-aged breakfast cereal, pioneering several forms of product promotion, he was not the first. The first actual advertise-ment campaign for breakfast cereals was created by the founder of Quaker Oats, Henry Crowell, who made an innovative advertising move with his product's packaging. In 1877, decades before Post or Kellogg, Crowell established the first trademarked product image with the easily recognizable figure of a Quaker on his boxes of rolled oats. There were health-based reasons for packaging food – the theory of germs was becoming popular during the 1870s and 1880s, and packaged foods seemed safer than unsealed bulk grains. Before Crowell's invention, cardboard packages of foods and other products would have only had the name of the product, perhaps with a slogan, on them. Crowell's new cardboard packages themselves became an area on which to place the brand's name and information about the product, as well as eye-catching pictures. Crowell's image of a Quaker brought with it associations of honesty, purity and a nostalgia for the early founders of the United States such as Benjamin Franklin. Quaker Oatmeal became a popular food in the late nineteenth century, thanks in large part to Crowell's marketing strategies, and it has remained so ever since.

Grape-Nuts advertisement, *c.* 1920.

Soon cereal companies had developed the now-ubiquitous brightly coloured cardboard cereal box to make their packaging as eye-catching, memorable and informative as possible. Cereal companies took advantage of captive audiences by providing entertainment on, and eventually in, their ready-to-eat cereal boxes. There were often jokes, cartoons, games for children, or short narratives – a development, perhaps, from the early promotional materials and health claims placed on boxes of cereals such as Post Grape-Nuts. Puzzles, crosswords and other kinds of games also appeared on cereal boxes. This trend largely faded in the late twentieth century – with the advent of television and, more recently, mobile phones, boxes have had too much competition in consumer entertainment. However, in 2014 in the United States, General

Mills designed a series of nostalgic cereal boxes for Cheerios, Honey Nut Cheerios, Lucky Charms, Cocoa Puffs and Cinnamon Toast Crunch. In addition to retro designs on the front of the boxes, these packages also included games and puzzles on the back, as cereal boxes from the 1950s through the 1990s would have had on them. As part of the campaign, General Mills included a $5 (roughly £3) coupon for similarly nostalgic Hasbro board games: Scrabble, Clue (Cluedo), Parcheesi and Risk. The companies – cereal and board game – made this connection: as families sit at the table eating cereal, they could likewise be sitting together playing board games.[3]

Breakfast cereal companies also developed mascots to help promote their products. The first breakfast cereal mascot was developed in 1902 for Force cereal, a wheat-based flake cereal that competed with Grape-Nuts, Corn Flakes, Shredded Wheat and Cream of Wheat for the North American and, later, European breakfast cereal market. This character was a cartoon figure called Sunny Jim. Scott Bruce and Bill Crawford call the character, 'a strutting grandfatherly gentleman in top hat, high collar and red-tailed coat, who wore his hair in a pigtail and carried a walking stick'. Minnie Maud Hanff developed a corresponding jingle for the Sunny Jim advertisements – also a breakfast cereal first. An unhappy, unlucky man, Jim Dumps begins eating Force cereal, and 'Since then they've called him "Sunny Jim".'[4] Like the Quaker before him, Sunny Jim became a widely recognizable figure. This Force campaign was wildly popular, and the fictional Sunny Jim became a celebrity. The only problem for the Force Company was that – as marketing campaigns have known ever since – the character of Sunny Jim did not, in fact, help with sales of Force cereal. The cereal remained unpurchased. Force lost popularity early in the United States and by the 1920s was not in contention against the Kellogg, Post and Quaker corporations. However, the cereal remained popular in the UK for much longer, into the 2010s, with Sunny Jim always remaining the mascot for the brand.

Another famous example is the team of Snap, Crackle and Pop, the first breakfast cereal mascot(s) of the Kellogg company. They started appearing in Rice Krispies advertisements in 1933, personifying the sound that Rice Krispies make when milk is added. According to the company website, in the 1950s a Spanish-language version of the advertisements helped sell *arroz tostadito* to global markets. Soon mascots abounded in the United States and across the world, as seen in the 1952 campaign introducing Tony the Tiger, in which he proclaimed that 'Sugar Frosted Flakes are Grrr-reat!' The slogan, 'They're Grrr-reat' became more famous in the United States, perhaps, than the cereal that it advertises. Mascots vary, as well, according to their country and region. In the UK, Weetabix Food Company developed Weetos, a chocolate breakfast cereal represented by the character Professor Weeto

Box of Force cereal, depicting mascot Sunny Jim, *c.* 1930s.

'The Road to Wellville', promotional pamphlet, c. 1900.

IF YOU have the slightest ambition to "Do things" in this world, to enjoy the keenest delights of Power, Money, Fame, and the perfect poise of Health, by all means get your feet on the "Road to Wellville."

Published by
POSTUM CEREAL CO., LTD.,
Battle Creek, Mich.
COPYRIGHTED

– a lab-coat-wearing elderly scientist, who helped reinforce the idea of the healthfulness of the cereal he promoted. He was the mascot for Weetos from the 1990s until 2010, at which time he was replaced by Weeto, a more generic cartoon character. In Latin America, the figure representing Kellogg's Choco Krispis is Melvin the elephant. The Swiss company Nestlé sells a chocolate breakfast cereal called Chocapic in Europe and Latin America, and its mascot is a dog named Pico. The same cereal is called Koko Krunch in

Asia and most of the Middle East, and uses Koko the Koala as its mascot.[5]

Mascots were not the only marketing strategy for breakfast cereal companies. In the early twentieth century, C. W. Post included booklets, titled 'The Road to Wellville', inside boxes of Grape-Nuts that detailed his story of regaining his own health through a diet that included cold breakfast cereal. Other cereal companies followed suit, including stories and recipes in their ready-to-eat cereals as well. In the 1870s the American Cereal Company, the parent company of Quaker Oats, provided recipe books with suggestions of alternative ways to prepare not only breakfast cereal, but other foods with their products, such as a 'Quaker Bread'.

Later, in the 1920s, Quaker Oats gave crystal radio sets, designed to be placed on top of cereal boxes, to more than a million customers. Collectibles started to become popular marketing gimmicks in all breakfast cereals, taking the place of the inserts of coupons and recipe books that had been part of breakfast cereal marketing in the late nineteenth and early twentieth centuries. The first cereal box toy prize was a button in a Kellogg's Pep cereal box in 1945. Soon, injection

Children's toys placed in cereal boxes – a popular marketing technique.

moulding made it easier and cheaper to create relatively small plastic toys. The possibilities were almost limitless for cereal companies from that point. Small plastic ships and cars, pinball machines and whistles were popular early cereal box toys across North America and Europe.[6]

In 1926 Wheaties created the first 'singing commercial' broadcast on the radio station WCCO in Minneapolis, Minnesota, the home of General Mills, titled 'Have you tried Wheaties?'. In addition, the 'original singing cowboy, Gene Autry, crooned for Quaker on his CBS radio series, *Melody Ranch*', which ran in the United States in the 1940s and '50s. This was the beginning of radio advertising, which would eventually lead to television advertisements, as well as advertising on the Internet and via social media in the 2020s.[7]

In another example, in 1932 a Chicago radio station began playing a show about a little boy named Skippy who goes on numerous adventures, with Wheaties promotions placed within the programme. However, the show was not without controversy – an episode of Skippy had to be pulled in 1932. In the episode, one of Skippy's friends is kidnapped. Unfortunately, it was aired in the same week in which Charles Augustus Lindbergh Jr, the son of Charles Lindbergh, famous worldwide for being the first man to fly solo across the Atlantic in 1927, was kidnapped and held for ransom. The public eagerly followed the story of the 'Lindbergh baby', hoping for baby Charles's safe return, but everyone was devastated when, despite the Lindberghs having paid the ransom, Charles was never returned to his parents, having, it later turned out, been killed during the initial abduction. It is unsurprising, then, that the show had to be cancelled due to the sensitivity of the subject at that time.[8]

Radio commercials inevitably led to television and film advertisements. Bruce and Crawford quote U.S. advertising executive William Morris as saying, in 1949, 'Television has the impact of an atom bomb.' Breakfast cereal companies – as some of the largest marketers in the world – wanted to take full advantage of that developing technology. *The Singing Lady*, developed by Kellogg's own advertising agency in 1948, was the first cereal-sponsored television show, an expansion of the radio show of the same name. In the 1950s, popular shows such as *Howdy Doody* and *The Adventures of Superman* (the George Reeves version) promoted specific breakfast cereals on their shows. In the early 1960s, Bullwinkle Moose promoted the Trix rabbit, and a rabbit has been a character in the Bullwinkle-themed show *Rocky and His Friends*. Meanwhile, Asia-Pacific is the fastest-growing breakfast cereal market, and in the 2010s, the Australian Weet-Bix brand of cereal became popular in China after being shown on a well-known Chinese television programme, *Ode to Joy*. This is one example of a trend that will only intensify in the future as breakfast cereals are aggressively marketed to China and the rest of the Asia-Pacific region.[9]

Other breakfast cereal promotions include sponsorship of events, or the licensing of popular children's shows or characters like Mickey Mouse. In the United States, Wheaties's parent company, General Mills, hit upon its lasting marketing strategy in the 1930s, when they started sponsoring Minneapolis minor league baseball games with a billboard that read 'Wheaties – Breakfast of Champions'. In 1935 Post Toasties licensed Mickey Mouse to be on their cereal boxes and commercials; Mickey Mouse, though, is only one famous character in a long list to have been included in a marketing campaign seen by customers throughout the world. In 1982 Donkey Kong, the first video-game-themed cereal, was developed. The Saudi Arabian cereal company SweeToon made a Sonic the Hedgehog cereal limited to that region in the

2010s. Meanwhile, Sonic the Hedgehog was also used as a tie-in with Kellogg's Frosted Flakes (Frosties in the UK) and General Mills' Cheerios, while Pokémon was used to promote General Mills cereals. At the height of its popularity, in the 2000s, the game *Guitar Hero* was used in a promotion for Kellogg's cereals; *Angry Birds* was linked to Cocoa Krispies; and *Skylanders* tied in with General Mills cereals. Recently the company Funko has developed nostalgic cereals as tie-ins to its Funko pop toys, in a kind of reverse marketing strategy – in this case, a toy comes with a breakfast cereal surprise.[10]

Breakfast cereal companies took advantage of the popularity of the new technology of television – specifically, of the advent of Saturday morning cartoons – to market their breakfast cereals directly to children. According to Heather Arndt Anderson: 'Once television was mainstream, breakfast cereals could be advertised during Saturday morning cartoons, when kids were not only a captive audience, but one likely to be without adult supervision.'[11] Across the globe, companies have marketed food and beverages – including sugary breakfast cereals – to children and adolescents more than to adults. In the 1970s, after studies had shown that the consumption of sugary cereals and other foods was connected to childhood obesity, the U.S. Federal Trade Commission tried unsuccessfully to stop companies from using cartoon characters in commercials for sugary ready-to-eat cereals. Another attempt to encourage companies to voluntarily stop using popular characters to market sugary breakfast cereals to children in 2009 also failed. Voluntary regulation by breakfast cereal companies has been largely unsuccessful across the Americas and Europe.

The development of yet another technology, the Internet, has made advertising sugary foods and drinks to children yet more challenging to regulate. The United Kingdom's

Perhaps the most colourful sugary breakfast cereal option: Froot Loops.

Committee on Advertising Practice included 'non-broadcast media' – such as the Internet – in their ban on the marketing of foods high in fat, salt and sugar to children. In the 2010s in the United States, the United States Department of Agriculture (USDA) enacted a local school wellness policy as part of their national school lunch programme, in which local educational agencies would have to establish guidelines regarding school meal standards, in an effort to reduce childhood obesity.[12]

In the twenty-first century, and with the popularity of social media, marketing strategies have taken on a more per-formative element. In 2011 the company Dare Vancouver designed a promotion in which a 6-metre-high (20 ft) box of the breakfast cereal Crunchy O's opened on a street in Vancouver, Canada, revealing its 'toy surprise', a Honda Civic. This advertisement for Honda plays on the marketing genius of breakfast cereals. In 2013 Dubai set a Guinness World Record for the largest cereal breakfast in an event sponsored

Cereal Killer Café, London.

by Kellogg Company of the Middle East and Africa. A total of 1,354 people ate Kellogg's cereal together. At the same event, the Kellogg Company won the record for largest cereal box, as well as one for the longest table to seat the crowd – at 301 metres (988 ft). By 2016 the Guinness World Record was for 1,852 people at an event in Zahle, Lebanon, sponsored by the Daher International Food Company/Poppins.

More recently, Weetabix sparked an Internet sensation in 2021 by posting on Twitter an image of Weetabix topped with Heinz beans – a play on the British classic dish of beans on toast. A host of celebrities, as well as the Twitter accounts of other food companies, weighed in, offering opinions on this take on a traditional breakfast cereal being prepared in a novel way. Since all publicity is good publicity, this free advertising can only have helped both Weetabix and Heinz beans. To some extent, this has always been the case, as seen in product sponsorships of sports and other community-based events, as well as gimmicks like sending boxes of cereal to soldiers in the Second World War and on adventures such as Edmund Hillary's Mount Everest expedition.[13]

Straddling the line between business marketing and, perhaps, an art installation, in the 2010s there emerged a new trend in dining – the breakfast cereal café. In 2014 a cereal-themed restaurant opened in London called Cereal Killer, serving a nostalgic variety of ready-to-eat breakfast cereals to a largely adult clientele. Other cafés have included Cereality (Houston, TX), Mix N' Munch (Pasadena, CA), Black Milk Cereal (Manchester, England), Cereal Lovers (Madrid, Spain), Pop Cereal Café (Lisbon, Portugal), Bol and Bagel (Clermont-Ferrand, France), Cereal Anytime (Melbourne, Australia) and Cereal Killers South Africa (Durban, South Africa). Whether these eateries are a passing fad or a sign of a new trend in dining and that elusive 'third space' (somewhere other than home or work) remains to be seen.

Arthur Rackham, 'Somebody has been at my porridge, and has eaten it all up!', illustration from Flora Annie Steel, *English Fairy Tales* (1922).

5

Breakfast Cereal
in Art and Culture

This shade of yellow, the color of my dress that
I am wearing when I was two years old, was the same
shade of yellow as boiled cornmeal, a food that my
mother was always eager for me to eat in one form
(as a porridge) or another (as fongie, the starchy
part of my midday meal) because it was cheap and
therefore easily available . . .

Jamaica Kincaid, 'Biography of a Dress' (1992)

Cereal has always been culturally significant, represented in
both high and popular art. Since ancient times, porridges
have found representation in culture. In addition, ready-to-
eat breakfast cereals quickly became iconic and representative
enough culturally to be represented, satirized and critiqued in
art. In her short story, 'Biography of a Dress' (1992), Jamaica
Kincaid associates the porridges of her childhood with rou-
tine, tradition and deprivation.[1] The mother's love for her
child is shown in her choice of foods – providing healthy
porridges for her. However, the daughter wants to rebel
against the ubiquity of cornmeal – seen here in both breakfast porridge and as lunch *fongie*. She longs for meat, as well
as other foods that are difficult for her mother to obtain due

to their expense. This chapter endeavours to give a sampling of some of the ways that cereals – porridges as well as ready-to-eat – are incorporated into art and culture. Throughout the world, regionally iconic cereals are represented in literature, visual arts, festivals and other outputs.

Literature

Canadian author Margaret Atwood describes a dystopian future in *MaddAddam* (2013). At one point in the novel, a character nostalgically remembers a ready-to-eat breakfast cereal called Choco-Nutrino, 'a desperate stab at a palatable breakfast cereal for children after the world chocolate crop had failed. It was said to contain burnt soy.' This play on the processed nature of cold breakfast cereals is expanded on later in the scene: 'The Choco-Nutrinos are in a bowl. They're like tiny pebbles, brown and alien-looking, granules from Mars. People used to eat this kind of stuff all the time, she thinks. They took it for granted.' While the cereal is not a favoured food, the fact of its existence at all makes it nostalgia-laden for the characters who find the box. Meanwhile, in Atwood's first novel, *The Edible Woman* (1969), the protagonist must economize her time to get ready in the morning, and this takes a toll on her breakfast choices. 'I had to skip the egg and wash down a glass of milk and a bowl of cold cereal which I knew would leave me hungry long before lunch-time.' In this instance, breakfast cereal is not nostalgic, but rather disappointing. The character already feels the future hunger even while she eats her breakfast – that supposedly important first meal of the day – of cereal. Encouragingly, Atwood has spoken of her love of breakfast – calling it the most 'hopeful' meal of the day. She notes that breakfast is a time when we 'don't yet know what atrocities the day may choose to visit upon us'. A bright-eyed innocence – even if partially ironic – greets Atwood's lived experiences with breakfast, and to some extent this concept is challenged and tinkered with in her fiction.[2]

On the other side of the planet, Australian novelist Liane Moriarty describes Weet-Bix as the quintessential, and therefore underwhelming, Australian breakfast cereal in *What Alice Forgot* (2009). In the book, the character Alice bemoans her bland persona: 'if only her parents could have been immigrants, with accents. Alice could have been bilingual and her mother could have made her own pasta. Instead, they were just the plain old suburban Jones family. As bland as Weet-Bix.' The way to rebel against middle-class Australian society, to be more interesting, she imagines, is to eat a breakfast cereal other than Weet-Bix, perhaps a savoury porridge. This is something the character doesn't do. Similarly, in Moriarty's later novel, *The Husband's Secret* (2013), a mother mourns her daughter every year on the anniversary of her death. This goes on for many years.

> She looked at her watch. It was only just after eight a. m. There were still hours and hours to endure before the day was done. At this time twenty-eight years ago, Janie had been eating her very last breakfast. Half a Weet-Bix, probably. She'd never liked breakfast.

In this case, it's the ubiquity of Weet-Bix that adds to the tragedy, a kind of melancholy. Instead of breakfast cereal being comforting, the thought of a dead loved one's final breakfast is decidedly painful, even after many years. But this is a particularly poignant pain because of the normalcy of a Weet-Bix breakfast, that normalcy being part of what lends to its tragedy.[3]

Porridges are also strongly represented in world literature. In the United States, maize-based porridges took on a national cultural significance in the early federal period, as a way for the new nation to mark itself against Great Britain. Often these porridges were eaten for breakfast, but just as often they were eaten at other times of the day. Joel Barlow describes a maize porridge in his mock-epic, 'The Hasty-Pudding, A Poem' (1796).

First in your bowl the milk abundant take,
Then drop with care along the silver lake
Your slakes of pudding; these at first will hide
Their little bulk beneath the swelling tide;
But when their growing mass no more can sink,
When the soft island looms above the brink,

A. & C. Kaufmann, *The Breakfast*, 1873, chromolithograph.

Then check your hand; you've got the portion's due,
So taught our sires, and what they taught is true.[4]

While the poem is a mock-epic, following Alexander Pope's style, and Barlow is not as celebratory of the maize mush as it seems on the surface, the fact remains that maize porridge is established as a foundational food representative of the United States shortly after nationhood. The maize-based hasty pudding was also made famous in 'Yankee Doodle', the song from the nation's Revolutionary War period. From this point, maize porridge in the form of hasty pudding, grits or hominy would be associated with the United States in particular – and specifically with the southern states.

Toni Morrison presented the suspense of her main character through his appetite towards the end of *Song of Solomon* (1977): 'Hungry as he was, he couldn't eat much of Vernell's breakfast, so he pushed the scrambled eggs, hominy, fried apples around in the plate, gulped coffee and talked a lot.' Hominy is made into part of a traditional breakfast that also includes eggs and apples. However, the main character does not have the appetite for this comforting breakfast food at a pivotal moment in the novel's plot. As in the case of the maize porridges described earlier in the nation's history, the hominy described in this novel is important given its regional specificity.[5]

Throughout Latin America, as well, the most important grain for porridges is maize. Thus it is unsurprising that perhaps the best-known poet from Latin America, the Chilean Pablo Neruda, wrote an 'Ode to Maize'. In this poem, he celebrates the process of making maize into the foods that have kept civilizations healthy for millennia: 'There, milk and matter,/ strength-giving, nutritious/ corn-meal pulp,/ you were worked and patted/ by the wondrous hands/ of dark-skinned women.' This poem celebrates both the porridge which could then be prepared into hominy-like breakfast cereals and other maize-based food preparations, as well as the indigenous women who have prepared it since ancient times. While Neruda's poem does not necessarily focus on the breakfast meal of a hominy form of maize, his paean to maize remains a significant one. This theme is seen throughout many Latin American cultures.[6]

In Chinese novels, meanwhile, the porridge being described is a rice-based congee. In one of the four classic Chinese texts, *The Dream of the Red Chamber*, written by Cao Xueqin and first printed in 1791, a woman uses the opportunity of preparing congee and other delicate foods to comfort a man in distress: 'Lady Feng . . . with her own hands, prepared, in the other mansion, every kind of fine congee and luscious small dishes, which she sent over, in order that he might be tempted to eat.'[7] In this scene, congee is shown in a very similar manner to congee in contemporary China. It is a comfort food – one that can be eaten at breakfast as a porridge or throughout the day if someone is feeling unwell.

Stories and poems for children also often use breakfast cereals as significant themes. The British fairy tale 'Goldilocks and the Three Bears', based on the Robert Southey original, 'The Story of the Three Bears' (1837), which starred an old woman rather than a young girl, uses porridge as one of the three trials of the tale, the third bear's porridge being, famously, 'just right'. In the original story, the bears had originally left their home to go for a walk and allow their bowls of breakfast porridge to cool before eating them. This tale has become one of the best-known stories in the English language.

The Czechs have a play poem that parents sing and perform with their children – akin to 'This Little Piggy' – called

'Vařila myšička kašičku', or 'Mother Mouse Cooked Porridge'. The lines of the song translate as, 'Mother mouse cooked porridge/ In a little green pan'; it goes on to count off each mouse who received its porridge, the final mouse receiving none and running to the cupboard for sugar instead. The words from this breakfast-cereal-themed song correspond with finger movements. The adults move their fingers on the palms of the children in a circle, as if stirring porridge. They then count off the fingers that represent the different baby mice receiving porridge. By the time they get to the fourth finger, or last mouse – the one who doesn't get any – they wiggle their fingers and 'run and run' up the children's arms until they tickle their armpits.[8]

Visual Arts

Breakfast cereals have long been culturally important beyond literature. The visual arts are equally concerned with the significance of breakfast cereal and with using or repurposing cereal and its paraphernalia. In the 1960s, Andy Warhol produced a Kellogg's Corn Flakes art installation – silk screen over wood – in conjunction with a Heinz Ketchup art series. As with his Campbell's soup can series, he comments on mass production and commodification through the repetition of the iconic u.s. breakfast cereal. Indeed, brand names themselves are, in many ways, the subject of his artworks.

In the twenty-first century, New York City-based artist Sarah Rosado creates art, including portraiture, using breakfast cereal. In some ways echoing the themes of Warhol's work, Rosado has made portraits of celebrities: among others, Beyoncé using Corn Flakes and Nicki Minaj using Fruity Pebbles. Other artistic representations of breakfast cereal include the work of Mohawk artist Greg A. Hill, from Ontario, Canada. He built a fully waterproof breakfast cereal box canoe and rowed it in his art installation *Portaging Rideau, Paddling the Ottawa to Kanata*. Canadian street artist Elicser Elliot has also turned to cereal boxes as a medium. His cereal box paintings represented U.S. and Canadian society during 2020 – with fears around police brutality and the COVID-19 pandemic, the world seemed to be out of sorts. These artistic efforts reinforce the importance of breakfast cereal in current times.

Paintings and other works of art show the European interest in breakfast cereal as well. The French artist Jean-François Millet created the etching *Cooling the Porridge* in 1861. It shows a mother blowing on a spoonful of porridge before feeding her child. Millet was part of the Realism movement, perhaps seen most clearly in his painting *The Gleaners*, and this

Jean-François Millet, *Cooling the Porridge*, 1861, etching.

Carl Larsson, 'Breakfast under the Big Birch', from *A Home* (1895), watercolour.

realism is seen in the details of the black-and-white porridge etching. Porridge can be seen here as being part of the bond between mother and child, the source of sustenance even after breastfeeding has finished.

Elsewhere in Europe, perhaps Sweden's most famous painter, Carl Larsson, also used a domestic scene involving porridge for one of his watercolours during the nineteenth century. His 1895 work *Breakfast under the Big Birch: From a Home* shows the Larsson family eating their morning meal together. The family itself – including the family dog – obscures the viewer from seeing the food on the table. However, the smallest girl (believed to be the artist's daughter, Brita) turns to face the viewer holding a cereal spoon. The tranquil scene coloured in reds, blues, greens and neutrals is representative of Larsson's focus on domestic life and harmony as part of the Swedish Arts and Crafts movement. Once again, the porridge-sharing of a family at breakfast is one of the comforting scenes of family life. In images like these,

Wooden lidded vessel, 19th century.

porridge in its various forms is shown as a breakfast cereal as well as a comfort food; there is little that is more comforting than nourishment among family and friends.

In television, a popular British show called *Porridge*, the slang term for a prison sentence – based on the simple breakfasts served in British prisons between the nineteenth and twentieth centuries – originally aired in 1974. The show takes place within a prison and follows the character Norman Stanley Fletcher, a habitual criminal. *Porridge* is a relatively light-hearted sitcom despite its setting in a prison environment. It was made into multiple specials and movies, as well as a 2017 television programme focusing on the son of the original character. This popular programme has not seemed to find success outside of Britain, though. Indeed, other countries have tried to remake the show, but these versions have never worked as well as the original British sitcom.

One work of African visual art that focuses on cereal is a lidded vessel, considered to be a porridge pot, of the Nguni people from the nineteenth century. The vessel is carved from a single piece of wood, with a separate piece for the lid. There are intricate details across its surface, showing that this pot would most likely have been intended to be a work of art in addition to – or perhaps instead of – a serviceable pot for carrying one of the most sustaining of the world's foods. Indeed, the form of the vessel is held by an artistic super-structure comprising a pedestal, legs, handles and a band around its centre. The scoring follows the overall shape of the vessel and might be meant to represent the weaving of fabric. Whether eaten as a warm breakfast cereal, or throughout the day, porridge is important enough to warrant being the subject of works of art for the Nguni community.

Festivals

Throughout the United States and Canada, agricultural fairs and harvest festivals have held prominent places in culture. In the United States, the national Cereal Fest occurs annually in Battle Creek, Michigan, the birthplace of modern breakfast cereal, sponsored by the original local breakfast cereal companies, Kellogg and Post. The festival's events and activities are housed in Kellogg Arena, and there is a corresponding parade that runs through the city, along with vendors and other entertainments. By showcasing an annual festival held during Michigan's summer season, Battle Creek takes advantage of its breakfast cereal fame to highlight the region.

National Thanksgiving holidays emphasize the native maize in addition to squash, beans and plentiful harvests in general. Set in the autumn, around the time of harvest and agricultural plenty, Thanksgiving takes place at the end of November in the United States and mid-October in Canada. Families and friends join together to celebrate the harvest and give thanks. While these are usually midday or evening meals, not breakfasts, the foods that make up the region's iconic porridges are well represented in these celebratory feasts.

Breakfast cereal festivals abound across Europe as well. There is an annual porridge festival in Scotland, the 'Golden Spurtle World Porridge Making Championship', named after a Scottish wooden kitchen implement used to stir oat porridge. This has become an annual competition for the best oat porridge preparation, the award being the eponymous golden spurtle. This festival started in 1994 and has become a draw for tourism to the region. It also celebrates World Porridge Day, 10 October, and has connections to local food banks and other charities.

Meanwhile, China has a congee-themed celebration called the Festival of Laba – the Eighth Day of the Twelfth lunar month – in which people line up in the morning at participating temples to receive the 'Eight Treasures' congee, made of rice, beans, fruits and nuts. These foods are symbolic and functional: they represent the foods left over at the end of winter – the heartiest and most basic of grains, dried fruits and nuts. These are then added together to make a sustaining congee. One legend behind this festival involves the celebration of Buddha reaching enlightenment at the age of 35, around the fifth century BCE. He was starving himself as a way to reach enlightenment, but he came to realize that starvation was not the path he sought. At that moment, a young woman offered him a simple congee dish, which he ate gratefully. To celebrate this, Chinese citizens, as well as tourists, line up early in the morning to celebrate by having a bowl of this satisfying congee for their breakfast.

The author's Eight Treasures/Laba congee, 2021.

Similarly, in Turkey, many families celebrate the Day of Ashura by making *ashure* pudding, a porridge made of barley, chickpeas, white beans, dried fruits, nuts and spices. The legend behind this porridge connects it to Noah's ark. Towards the end of their journey, when their supplies were mostly gone, Noah's family combined whatever was left into *ashure*, celebrating the appearance of Mount Ararat. Today this pudding porridge is a celebratory food eaten throughout the day, shared among friends and neighbours.

Other Cultural Outputs

In 2013 the Museum of Food and Drink in New York City created 'BOOM! The Puffing Gun and the Rise of Breakfast Cereal' as one of its first exhibits. The museum demonstrated the technology behind breakfast cereal, specifically the puffing gun's role in literally shaping the industry with such dominant cereals as Kix, Cheerios and Corn Pops. This exhibit parallels one of the earliest demonstrations of the puffing gun, at the Louisiana Purchase Exposition world's fair in St Louis, Missouri, in 1904, where Alexander Anderson first puffed rice for excited onlookers for American Cereal Company, also known as Quaker Company.

In 2007 Weetabix joined with the Weetabix Growers Group in the UK to host a competition for creating Weetabix sculptures out of hay bales on local farms. Examples of entries included a bear eating a bowl of Weetabix, a scene of popular characters Wallace and Gromit with Weetabix boxes and a tractor pulling giant boxes of Weetabix. This competition was, in part, used to draw attention to the company's commitment to obtaining their grain from within 80 kilometres (50 mi.) of their factory. This highlights the company's positive impacts, as well as adding whimsy to the local region.

UNESCO placed Mexican cuisine on their Representative List of the Intangible Cultural Heritage of Humanity in 2010 for its focus on the trio of maize, beans and chilli, as well as traditional farming techniques, processing techniques such as nixtamalization or the preparation of maize in an alkaline solution, and the cultural symbolism of food as seen in the offerings that occur during the Día de los Muertos festival on 1 November. While not a harvest festival focused on maize per se, Mexico's Día de los Muertos traditionally involves drinking *atole*, a spiced maize porridge consumed as a beverage. *Atole* is made with maize masa (ground hominy flour), water, sugar, cinnamon and optional vanilla, chocolate or other spices. It is served as a cosy and rich drink to be consumed during autumn evenings such as on 1 November. As maize is one of the foundational cereal grains throughout human civilization, and as it was developed and originally cultivated in what is now Mexico, the importance of cereals in the form of maize-based porridges on Mexican culture is difficult to overstate. The various maize

porridges demonstrate its significance in Mexican breakfasts, as well as in its culture overall.

The maize porridge known as *nsima* was added to the UNESCO Intangible Cultural Heritage List in 2017, as part of the culinary traditions of Malawi. This thick porridge is known by other regional names such as *pap*, *fufu* (and its myriad of spellings), *mieliepap*, *sadza* and *ugali*, among others. The porridge requires specific preparation styles, which have been passed between elders and the younger generations. The pounding of *nsima* and its porridge relatives is bound up in traditional ways of life. It's a safeguarded knowledge held by the communities in the form of continual practice and regional festivals. A culinary staple, variations can be prepared as a starch for a midday meal, with meats or other savoury additions for the evening meal or, especially, warmed as a porridge for breakfast.

Speaking of *pap*, in South Africa in 2015, Nwabisa Mda, Thembe Mahlaba and Bongeka Masango created a YouTube channel called *Pap Culture* that, by the early 2020s, had over a million views, more than 10,000 subscribers and a variety of critical notices. The entertainment channel has published new episodes every Wednesday, focusing on questions that matter to South African youth. Their goal, as stated on their YouTube page, has been to allow viewers 'to indulge in a good long laugh' and 'open up dialogue about things that matter to young people'. It's fitting that a channel focusing on South African culture – and perhaps especially on youth – uses the national porridge in its name.

6
The Future(s) of Breakfast Cereal

In many ways breakfast cereal is the prototypical processed food:
four cents' worth of commodity corn (or some other equally
cheap grain) transformed into four dollars' worth of
processed food. What an alchemy!

Michael Pollan, *Omnivore's Dilemma* (2006)

Breakfast cereals have a long and distinguished, and surprising,
history. It is an interesting challenge, then, to imagine their
future. Will cereals develop better, healthier flavour combinations, with more functionality? Will cold breakfast cereal
have a different outlook from traditional – and largely non-
branded – porridges? Michael Pollan's tirade against processed
foods takes careful aim at the 'alchemy' of ready-to-eat breakfast cereals in a way that might seem almost dystopian. The
fictional, rather than journalistic, dystopian ideas of future
breakfast cereals often return to porridges, as opposed to the
ready-to-eat kind, involving some kind of nutrition-rich functional paste. These neo-porridges lack in flavour but contain
basic nutrients that can successfully keep post-apocalyptic
communities healthy. This reimagining of the original porridges, which fed the Roman gladiators and Egyptian labourers,
as well as countless others throughout history, is also a play on

John Harvey Kellogg's invention of a pre-digested breakfast cereal. Science-fiction examples of these neo-porridges have appeared in such works as the film *The Matrix* (1999) and the zombie novel *Zone One* (2011), and of course there is the iconic nutrient-rich, cannibal porridge-gone-wrong of the film *Soylent Green* (1973). Dystopian tales aside, it's not possible to imagine just the one future for breakfast cereal. Rather, there could be any number of futures, based on certain trends that have started in recent years.

For much of the twentieth century, breakfast cereal companies made huge profits from their packaged foods. However, not all has remained financially solid in the breakfast cereal markets of the twenty-first century. There has been a new trend towards moving away even from the time it takes to pour a bowl of cereal and milk, to eat it and to clean up afterwards. As people have become even busier in their modern lives, they are giving themselves less time for breakfast. Busy families around the world are therefore looking for hand-held breakfast foods that can be eaten almost literally on the run.

Breakfast cereal companies have, of course, responded with new products to meet this new consumer desire. The development of breakfast cereal bars, referred to as granola bars or muesli bars (simplified from the original müesli), are one way that the breakfast cereal corporations are keeping up with modern society. In addition, these cereal bars make for handy snacks to eat between meals or while away from the table. Their convenience is a major factor in their favour. Unfortunately, these breakfast cereal bars are often as sugar-filled as sweets, and the 'wholegrains' involved are negated by other, unhealthy additional ingredients. Also, granola or muesli bars aren't necessarily fortified with vitamins and minerals in the same way that other ready-to-eat breakfast cereals are. Nevertheless, cereal bars have developed into a booming trend for food companies, and each of the major breakfast cereal corporations has a dedicated line of cereal bar brands. This trend will most likely grow in the future.

In the grocery store or supermarket, granola and muesli bars are usually marketed in the same aisle as other packaged breakfast cereals. The Kellogg Company has a line of Special K and Kashi protein bars, as well as 'snack bars' – made from sugary cereals such as Rice Krispies, Apple Jacks and Corn Pops. General Mills markets the Nature Valley granola bars, and Quaker Oats has a Quaker Chewy granola bar. Globally, Nestlé has an Uncle Toby's muesli bar. Interestingly, Post has not developed a granola or muesli bar corresponding to its most recognizable cereal brands. Meanwhile, some small-brand companies produce energy-filled cereal bars, as well. The Clif Bar company, which specializes in energy bars and other energy foods, rejected an offer to be purchased by Quaker Oats. According to the company website, they are

Granola bar ready for its close-up.

Cereal aisle, Taiwan. Note the Chinese characters on some of the cereals.

now also international, opening their markets to the UK in 2007. In every case, these are options for busy people who might not have time to prepare a meal even as simple as cold breakfast cereal.

Given the rise of other convenient breakfast foods, cereal no longer dominates the market. Breakfast cereal companies have been struggling to adapt in the twenty-first century. One way they are attempting to do this is through expanding the market to as-yet unconquered regions of the world, specifically the population hub of Asia-Pacific. North America and Europe have remained the dominant markets for breakfast cereals in the first quarter of the twenty-first century. How-ever, go into any supermarket in a major city in Asia-Pacific, such as Taipei, for example, and you will see a cereal aisle there. Note the differences in mascots, flavour combinations and languages. Asia-Pacific is a large enough market that all corporations are eagerly working to break into it – not just breakfast cereal companies. However, the region is largely one that eats more savoury breakfasts – dishes that traditionally consist of rice and soy sauce, fish and other meats. Convin-cing half of the world's population to entirely change their chosen breakfast foods has proven to be a daunting task. But, with a market that large, breakfast cereal corporations are aggressively working to do just that, and future breakfasts in Asia-Pacific may come to look more Western in the next few years.

Another way the breakfast cereal industry is working to increase its market share is by encouraging people to eat cer-eal at other times of the day besides the morning. University students, for example, eat cereal increasingly at any time of the day. Cereal is known to have vitamins, wholegrains and, with the addition of milk, protein. Thus it's often not the worst dietary choice a busy student might make. Increas-ingly, therefore, university cafeterias are including ready-to-eat breakfast cereals in their buffets – not just during scheduled dining times – along with milk dispensers. It's a comparably healthy snack or meal substitute for a busy student. In addi-tion, these students may continue to eat cereal at dinner, for example, when they become busy professionals. Thus break-fast will again become a meal that can be eaten at any time of the day, much as porridges have been historically.

The early inventors of breakfast cereal wanted to make foods easier to process and digest as part of their understand-ing of nutrition science. Modern nutritionists, though, have

Rice Krispie Treats, because breakfast cereal can make delightful desserts.

shown that the quick absorption of calories through the easy processing of foods is a large cause of the obesity epidemic in the United States and across the globe. The U.S. Center for Disease Control states that one in five children in the United States is obese. The World Health Organization corroborates this at the global scale, observing that between 1975 and 2016, childhood episodes of obesity and overweight increased from 4 per cent to 18 per cent worldwide. Indeed, more people are overweight than underweight in every region of the world except Sub-Saharan Africa and Asia. As developing countries become more Westernized in their diets, Western diseases are having higher rates of occurrence. A primary source of added sugars in U.S. diets, according to the USDA's dietary guidelines for 2020–25, is pre-sweetened breakfast cereals, which appear on a list that includes desserts, sweets and snacks. Breakfast cereals in this instance decidedly do not look like part of a balanced diet. The USDA's common-sense recommendation is to

Parfait, granola and yoghurt.

choose lower-sugar ready-to-eat cereals made with wholegrains. The USDA notes that wholegrain foods in general are consumed at lower than recommended levels. Though wholegrains are under-consumed, there is an overall overconsumption of grains, because of the consumption of refined grains. Ready-to-eat breakfast cereals, including porridges like oatmeal, are some of the primary sources of wholegrains for children and adolescents in the United States. These recommendations are suggested for toddlers through adults.[1]

Furthermore, there is a rising concern about emphasizing the functional foods aspect of cold breakfast cereals, or the idea that cereals have supplemental nutrients, making them superior foods, as had been the case throughout the twentieth century. Warren Belasco notes that viewing breakfast cereals as functional foods is risky behaviour. In 1999 the Grocery Manufacturers of America worried about applying science to food in terms of micronutrients. Belasco quotes the report, 'Today's research confirming the benefits of an ingredient or product may be invalidated or even reversed tomorrow.'[2] All too often, this is exactly what comes to pass. While there always seems to be a trendy micronutrient available in a supplement form, often developers lack enough knowledge about how that nutrient is absorbed and managed in the human body. A varied diet with more fruits, vegetables and wholegrains has consistently been found to be the healthiest, for breakfast or at any time of the day.

In addition to relating to health, in 2020 breakfast cereal made headlines once more in the United States. As the world was dealing with lockdowns and other disruptions brought about through the COVID-19 pandemic, there was a series of shortages of basic grocery items. Some of these shortages were sensible enough – antibacterial and cleaning products, for example. Perhaps one of the stranger items to vanish from grocery store shelves during this time, though, was Post Grape-Nuts. The increased demand for the humble but nostalgic breakfast cereal, and the reduced production due to COVID-19 precautions, left stock completely depleted. Determined consumers, though, developed a robust black-market trade in the cereal, buying boxes at elevated rates through online venues. Journalists struggled to understand why a seemingly bland staple like Grape-Nuts would have become so in demand during the pandemic. By spring 2021, the shortage had ended, and Post Consumer Brands, the parent company of Post Grape-Nuts, showed its appreciation for customer loyalty and perseverance through a series of coupons and prizes, announced on its corporate website.[3] While leading up to 2020, breakfast cereals had been in a financial decline, the pandemic drove sales, as consumers returned to eating breakfast at home and sought comforting foods. Indeed, this has been a long-held truth in the industry: breakfast cereals do well during periods of crisis, as W. K. Kellogg had discovered in the 1930s in the United States during the Great Depression with his own brand cereals.

Grape-Nuts, which faced a COVID-19-related shortage in 2020.

And so, the history of breakfast cereal looks to the future. Deeply connected to capitalism and multinational corporations, the 'get-rich-quick scheme' is an embedded element of the history of ready-to-eat breakfast cereals, and that impulse remains. However, its history includes the nobler aims of the era's health movements, reaction against the rapid increases of meat production and its health consequences, the desire for individual and cultural improvement and the science of nutrition. Ironically, John Harvey Kellogg and his competitors and followers wanted to make foods easier to digest as part of their understanding of nutrition science, a belief that has been completely negated by modern nutritionists. Of course, Kellogg would never have approved of the manner in which these new ready-to-eat breakfast cereals are being produced – with excessive amounts of sugar and highly processed flours. Ultimately, Kellogg and all who came after – not to mention the millions who prepared porridges before – would be satisfied to know that breakfast cereal in some way, shape or form isn't going anywhere. There will always be a need for comfort, for wholegrains, for that 'well-balanced' way to break one's fast and to start one's day off right.

Recipes

Early Breakfast Cereal Recipes

Corn Porridge
From Eliza Leslie, *Miss Leslie's New Cookery Book* (1857)

Take young corn, and cut the grains from the cob. Measure it, and to each heaping pint of corn allow not quite a quart of milk. Put the corn and milk into a pot, stir them well together, and boil them till the corn is perfectly soft. Then add some bits of fresh butter dredged with flour, and let it boil five minutes longer. Stir in at the last, four beaten yolks of eggs, and in three minutes remove it from the fire. Take up the porridge and send it to table hot, and stir some fresh butter into it. You may add sugar and nutmeg.

Quaker Breakfast Porridge
From the American Cereal Co.,
America's Cereal Foods and How to Cook Them (1894),
https://lib.msu.edu

Use a Double Kettle, then there is no danger of burning.

Always use *freshly boiling* water, not water that has stood in the tea-kettle all night.

Salt the water to taste before putting the Rolled Oats in.

Stir one part Quaker Oats into two parts *freshly boiling* water. Be careful to stir in slowly so that the porridge may be kept free from lumps and each grain thoroughly scalded. Boil twenty minutes to half an hour, and, if you can allow the time, let the porridge simmer on the stove for half an hour longer. It will have all the more flavour.

Do not stir at all while cooking if a double boiler is used. Keep your kettle covered. Milk can be used instead of water, if preferred or half milk and half water.

Serve hot with sugar and cream or syrup, as preferred.

Quaker Bread
The American Cereal Co., 'We Feed the World', in *Cereal Foods and How to Cook Them*, 4th edn (*c.* 1880)

To make one loaf of 'Quaker Oats Bread', set a sponge over night made of half a cake of yeast, dissolved in one and one-half cups warm water, and one and one-half cups sifted flour; in the morning take one cup Quaker Oats, pour over it one cup boiling water, two tablespoonfuls sugar, and a pinch of salt; add all to the sponge, and stir in wheat flour until it is as stiff as can be stirred with a spoon. Let it rise until light, and bake one hour.

Bircher Müesli
Adapted from Maximilian Bircher-Benner,
Fruit Dishes and Raw Vegetables: Sunlight (Vitamine) Food (1930),
trans. Reginald Snell (1985)

1 tablespoon of rolled oats, left to soak in 3 tablespoons of cold water for 12 hours
1 tablespoon of sweetened condensed milk and/or honey
½ tablespoon of lemon juice
1 large or 2 small apples, freshly grated with the skin on
1 tablespoon of ground hazelnuts or almonds

Soak oats in water over night. In the morning, grate the apple into the bowl with the oats. Stir in lemon juice. Add in nuts. Pour milk over müesli, then drizzle the honey on top of the milk.

Modern Old-Fashioned Granola
Adapted from Cookie and Kate, https://cookieandkate.com

360 g (4 cups) old-fashioned rolled oats
225 g (1½ cups) raw nuts and/or seeds
1 teaspoon sea salt
1 teaspoon ground cinnamon
120 ml (½ cup) olive oil, canola oil or coconut oil
120 ml (½ cup) maple syrup or honey
1 teaspoon vanilla extract
160 g (1 cup) dried fruit

Preheat oven to 180°C or 350°F and line large baking sheet with parchment paper. In a large bowl, mix together oats, nuts and/or seeds, salt and cinnamon. Pour in oil, maple syrup and/or honey and vanilla. Mix well, until everything is lightly coated. Spread granola evenly onto prepared baking sheet. Bake until lightly golden, 20 to 25 minutes roughly, stirring half-way. The granola will get crispier as it dries. Let the granola cool and dry completely, at least 45 minutes. Top with dried fruit. Break into pieces with your hands for larger chunks, or stir with a spoon for smoother granola. Store in airtight container for 1 to 2 weeks, or freeze for up to 3 months.

Slap Pap (Maize Meal Porridge)
– Breakfast Version of *Pap*
Adapted from Marietjie Swart and Jaco Swart,
www.rainbowcooking.co.nz

Slap pap is a smooth maize meal porridge served with milk for breakfast, with a little sugar and butter.

125 g (1 cup) maize meal
1 l (4 cups) water
1 teaspoon salt
1 tablespoon butter

Boil water and salt in a pot, covered with lid. Stir maize meal into the boiling water. Simmer for at least 30 minutes, in pot covered with lid. Add butter. Serve with optional milk and sugar or honey.

Korean Dakjuk/Congee
Adapted from Hyosun Bapsang, www.koreanbapsang.com

This porridge is delicious for breakfast or throughout the day as a snack or light meal – especially on cold winter days.

150 g (1 cup) short grain rice or glutinous rice
1.5 l (6 cups) chicken stock
1 medium carrot
1 medium celery stalk
4–6 button mushrooms
135 g (1 cup) pulled chicken, seasoned with salt, pepper and garlic
1–2 tablespoons sesame oil
spring onions, chopped (optional)
sesame seeds (optional)

Soak rice for 1 hour; drain. Chop vegetables. Add 1–2 tablespoons sesame oil to soup pot. Add the rice and sauté for 3–5 minutes over medium heat, until rice turns translucent. Add stock to pot and bring to a boil. Cook, stirring occasionally, for 20–25 minutes, until rice is fully cooked. Make sure rice isn't sticking to the bottom of the pot. Add vegetables, stir, cover and simmer for 10–15 minutes more, until vegetables are soft. Adjust consistency of porridge to taste by adding more stock or water. Stir in pre-cooked chicken at the end, leaving some to use as a garnish, if desired. Add salt and pepper to taste. Serve warm with optional garnishes on top.

Breakfast Cereal Recipes
for Festive Occasions

In some cultures, breakfast cereals are prepared as something more like a celebratory porridge or pudding. The following two examples can be served at breakfast or throughout the day as a dessert.

Laba Zhou, or Eight Treasures Congee
Adapted from Maggie Zhu, https://omnivorescookbook.com

150 g (1 cup) glutinous rice
100 g (¾ cup) combination of small red mung beans, black or brown rice
50 g (⅓ cup) combination of raisins, peanuts, cashews and/or dried jujubes
50 g (⅓ cup) combination of lotus seeds, pine nuts
75 g (½ cup) brown sugar
optional toppings: dried longan, other dried fruits or nuts as desired

Directions for pressure cooker
Add all dry ingredients, except sugar, and 2 litres (8 cups) water to the pressure cooker. Set to cook at high pressure for 25 minutes. When done, release pressure naturally (this is important to keep the glutinous rice from clogging the vent). Once pressure releases, stir congee to preferred consistency and add sugar to taste. Serve warm.

Directions for stove top
Soak glutinous rice, other rice, nuts and red beans in water in a large bowl overnight. Drain thoroughly before cooking. Combine soaked rice, nuts and beans with other ingredients in a large pot. Add 2.5 litres (10 cups) water. Cook over medium-high heat, bringing to a boil. Reduce heat to low and simmer covered (leave gap for steam to escape) for 40 minutes for a thin consistency or 60 minutes for a thicker consistency. Stir in sugar to taste and serve warm.

Ashure
Adapted from Elizabeth Taviloglu, www.thespruceeats.com

Technically, this cereal is not a breakfast cereal but rather a dessert. It's supposedly the cereal eaten by Noah and the rest of the ark inhabitants. After being on the ark for some time, they started running low on food, and threw everything into one pot and let it cook. The result was this delicious celebratory pudding/cereal.

400 g (2 cups) barley or wholegrain wheat, soaked overnight and drained
300 g (1 ½ cups) or 1 can chickpeas, rinsed and drained
300 g (1 ½ cups) or 1 can white beans, rinsed and drained
50 g (¼ cup) uncooked rice
3 tablespoons dried raisins, sultanas or currants
3 tablespoons pine nuts
95 g (½ cup) dried apricots, coarsely chopped
95 g (½ cup) dried figs, coarsely chopped
75 g (½ cup) almonds, walnuts, pistachios or peanuts, coarsely chopped
440 g (2 cups) sugar
1 cinnamon stick
zest from 1 orange
zest from 1 lemon
1 tablespoon rose water (optional)

Add chickpeas, beans, rice, dried fruits and nuts, cinnamon, sugar, zests and optional rose water to pre-cooked barley or other grain. Add more water to cover ingredients, if needed. Bring mixture to a boil. Cook, stirring occasionally, until mixture thickens, around 20 minutes. Remove *ashure* from heat and fill individual bowls or one large serving bowl. Cover and refrigerate for several hours. Serve with optional garnishes, such as additional pine nuts or pistachios or chopped dried fruits.

Sweet Recipes/Desserts

Ready-to-eat breakfast cereals started as health foods to be eaten first thing in the morning. However, as soon as they were packaged and marketed to the public, they became sweetened and associated with other sweet foods, like desserts. Their connection to dessert foods, therefore, is almost as well established as the history of cold breakfast cereal itself. The following examples represent breakfast-cereal-themed sweet treats from around the world.

Baked Apples with Grape-Nuts
From *Recipes: Highly Nutritious Dishes Easy to Make*, Postum Cereal Co. (1922), https://lib.msu.edu

6 level tablespoons Grape-Nuts or All-Bran Buds or other wheat bran cereal
6 apples (green apples preferred)
150 g (¾ cup) sugar
120 ml (½ cup) water
1 lemon (optional)

Wash and core the apples; place in baking dish and fill cavities with Grape-Nuts or alternative, sugar and few drops of lemon juice or place a slice of lemon on each apple. Pour the water into baking dish and bake in slow oven. When done, sprinkle with powdered sugar.

Grape-Nuts Ice Cream (No. 1)
From *Recipes: Highly Nutritious Dishes Easy to Make*, Postum Cereal Co. (1922), https://lib.msu.edu

120 g (1 cup) Grape-Nuts or All-Bran Buds or other wheat bran cereal
950 ml (1 quart) rich (double) cream

4 level tablespoons sugar
1 level teaspoon almond extract
1 level teaspoon vanilla extract

Scald 470 ml (1 pt) of the cream in a double boiler, and to this add, while hot, the Grape-Nuts or alternative and sugar. Stir well, and when cool, add the remaining cream and flavourings. Prepare in ice cream machine according to directions or place in freezer until frozen, usually around 3–4 hours, stirring occasionally. A tablespoon of sherry may take the place of the extracts, if desired.

Grape-Nuts Ice Cream (No. 2)
From *Recipes: Highly Nutritious Dishes Easy to Make*, Postum Cereal Co. (1922), https://lib.msu.edu

Start with prepared vanilla ice cream. Just before the cream congeals in freezing, add dry Grape-Nuts in the proportion of 1 cup to 3.75 litre (1 gal) of ice cream. This will retain the crispness of the granules, and they will give the cream a highly palatable, nut-like flavour.

Rice Krispie Treats
Adapted from Deb Perelman, *Smitten Kitchen*, https://smittenkitchen.com

170 g (¾ cup) unsalted butter, plus extra for pan
285 g (20 oz) mini marshmallows
¼ teaspoon sea salt
225 g (9 cups) crispy rice cereal

Butter/spray 23 × 33 cm (9 × 13 in.) pan or equivalent. In a large pot, melt butter over medium-low heat. Stir frequently, scraping up any bits from the bottom as you do. Pay attention, butter can burn easily. You want it a brown colour with a nutty scent, not burnt. As soon as the butter has taken on that nutty quality, turn heat off and stir in the marshmallows. Stir until marshmallows are smooth. Then stir in salt and cereal. Quickly spread into pan, making sure to press edges and corners in thoroughly. Allow to cool, at least 30 or 45 minutes. Then cut into squares and serve cool or at room temperature.

Weet-Bix Chocolate Chip Cookies
Adapted from Vanya Insull, https://vjcooks.com

150 g (⅔ cup) unsalted butter, softened
3 tablespoons vegetable oil
110 g (½ cup) brown sugar
2 tablespoons syrup (golden or maple – optional: substitute agave syrup)
60 ml (¼ cup) milk
200 g (1½ cup) all-purpose or plain flour
1 teaspoon baking powder
50 g (½ cup) rolled oats
¼ teaspoon salt
3 Weet-Bix (substitute Weetabix or Shredded Wheat)
160 g (1 cup) chocolate chips

Preheat oven to 180°C (350°F). Line a baking tray with parchment paper. In a large bowl, mix together softened butter, oil, brown sugar and syrup. Add the milk and mix. Sift in the flour and baking powder; then add the oats, salt and crushed Weet-Bix or alternative. Mix by hand to combine. Finally, stir in chocolate chips. Using a tablespoon, scoop out mixture into cookies, flattening slightly. Makes roughly 20 cookies. Bake approximately 8–10 minutes. Remove when golden brown. Cool on a rack. Cookies can be stored in an airtight container for one week.

References

Introduction

1 Rachel Laudan, *Cuisine and Empire: Cooking in World History* (Berkeley, CA, 2013), p. 314.
2 Antonia Affinita et al., 'Breakfast: A Multidisciplinary Approach', *Italian Journal of Pediatrics*, XXXIX/44 (2013), pp. 1–3.

1 Porridges around the World: Warm Breakfast Cereal

1 Catherine Zabinski, *Amber Waves: The Extraordinary Biography of Wheat, from Wild Grass to World Megacrop* (Chicago, IL, 2020), p. 62.
2 Andrew Dalby, *The Breakfast Book* (London, 2013), p. 25.
3 Heather Arndt Anderson, *Breakfast: A History* (New York, 2013), pp. 5–6.
4 Zabinski, *Amber Waves*, pp. 41–2.
5 Renee Marton, *Rice: A Global History* (London, 2014), pp. 30–35.
6 Not all maize grown is for human food, however; much of the maize grown globally is used for feed for livestock, as well as ethanol production in the United States.
7 Marton, *Rice*, p. 109.

8 Adrián Recinos, *Popul Vuh: A Sacred Book of the Ancient Quiché Maya*, trans. Delia Goetz and Sylvanus G. Morley (Norman, OK, 1950), p. 167.

9 Anderson, *Breakfast*, p. 34.

10 James C. McCann, *Stirring the Pot: A History of African Cuisine* (Columbus, OH, 2010), p. 204.

11 Anderson, *Breakfast*, p. 8.

12 Jane Austen, *Emma* [1815] (London, 1896), p. 88.

2 The Invention of Cold Breakfast Cereal

1 Heather Arndt Anderson, *Breakfast: A History* (New York, 2013), p. 17.

2 Scott Bruce and Bill Crawford, *Cerealizing America: The Unsweetened Story of American Breakfast Cereal* (Winchester, MA, 1995), p. xiv.

3 Anderson, *Breakfast*, p. 21.

4 Much of this information is based on original materials from the John Harvey Kellogg papers at Michigan State University (MSU) Archives and Historical Collections, box 5.

5 John Harvey Kellogg, *Flaked Cereals and Process of Preparing Same*, U.S.558393a, United States Patent Office (Washington, DC, 1896), lines 72–7.

6 MSU JH Kellogg papers, box 8.

7 Gerald Carson, *Cornflake Crusade* (New York, 1957), p. 162.

8 Bruce and Crawford, *Cerealizing America*, p. 38.

9 Anderson, *Breakfast*, p. 39.

3 Breakfast Cereal since the Nineteenth Century around the World

1 See Frank Fayant, 'The Industry that Cooks the World's Breakfast', *Success Magazine*, VI/108 (1903), p. 281.

2 Gerald Carson, *Cornflake Crusade* (New York, 1957), p. 6.

3 Heather Arndt Anderson, *Breakfast: A History* (New York, 2013), p. 39; Paul Griminger, 'Casimir Funk: A Biographical Sketch (1884–1967)', *Journal of Nutrition*, CII/9 (1972), pp. 1105–13; S. Sugasawa, 'History of Japanese Natural Product Research', *Pure and Applied Chemistry*, IX/1 (1964), pp. 1–20.

4 Scott Bruce and Bill Crawford, *Cerealizing America: The Unsweetened Story of American Breakfast Cereal* (Winchester, MA, 1995), pp. 103–4.

5 See www.sanitarium.com.au, www.weetbix.com.au and www.sanitarium.co.nz, accessed 22 August 2021.

6 Bruce and Crawford, *Cerealizing America*, pp. 243–6.

7 Anderson, *Breakfast*, pp. 38–9.

8 J. K. Rowling, *Harry Potter and the Philosopher's Stone* (London, 1997), pp. 8, 36.

9 J. K. Rowling, *Harry Potter and the Chamber of Secrets* (London, 1998), p. 68.

10 Derek Oddy and Derek S. Miller, 'The Consumer Revolution', in *The Making of the Modern British Diet*, ed. Derek Oddy and Derek S. Miller (London, 1976), p. 33.

4 Marketing and Breakfast Cereal

1 Saki (H. H. Munro), 'Filboid Studge', in *Humor, Horror, and the Supernatural: 22 Stories by Saki* (New York, 1977), p. 50.

2 Scott Bruce and Bill Crawford, *Cerealizing America: The Unsweetened Story of American Breakfast Cereal* (Winchester, MA, 1995), p. 28.

3 Lynne Morioka, 'Go Back in Time with Retro Cereal Boxes', General Mills, http://blog.generalmills.com, 26 February 2014.

4 Bruce and Crawford, *Cerealizing America*, pp. 40–41.

5 See www.ricekrispies.com, www.kelloggs.com, www.weetabixfoodcompany.co.uk, www.kelloggs.com.ar and www.nestle-cereals.com, accessed 21 October 2021.

6 Bruce and Crawford, *Cerealizing America*, p. 76; Heather Arndt Anderson, *Breakfast: A History* (New York, 2013), p. 23.

7 Bruce and Crawford, *Cerealizing America*, pp. 77–9.

8 Ibid., p. 82.

9 Ibid., p. 115. Julie Power, 'Soap Opera Ode to Joy propels Weet-Bix Push into China', *Sydney Morning Herald*, www.smh.com.au, 19 October 2016.

10 Bruce and Crawford, *Cerealizing America*, pp. 93–4; Anderson, *Breakfast*, pp. 181–2.

11 Anderson, *Breakfast*, p. 108.

12 Ibid. See also Adena Pinto et al., 'Food and Beverage Advertising to Children and Adolescents on Television: A Baseline Study', *International Journal of Environmental Research and Public Health*, XVII/6 (2020), available at www.mdpi.com; Sally Mancini and Jennifer Harris, 'Policy Changes to Reduce Unhealthy Food and Beverage Marketing to Children in 2016 and 2017', *Rudd Brief*, April 2018, https://uconnruddcenter.org; 'Local School Wellness Policy', USDA *Food and Nutrition Service*, 19 December 2019, www.fns.usda.gov.

13 Kevin Lynch, 'Record Trio for Dubai as City Tucks into the World's Largest Cereal Breakfast', Guinness World Records, www.guinnessworldrecords.com, 2 May 2013; Rachel Swatman, 'Cereal Brand Breaks Two World Records as Thousands Attend Group Breakfast in Lebanon', Guinness World Records, www.guinnessworldrecords.com, 12 October 2016; 'Honda Cereal Box', ADS Archive, https://adsarchive.com, accessed 15 April 2020; 'The Controversial Breakfast Twitter Can't Swallow', BBC Food, www.bbc.co.uk, accessed 30 March 2020.

5 Breakfast Cereal in Art and Culture

1 Jamaica Kincaid, 'Biography of a Dress', *Grand Street*, XI (1992), pp. 92–3.

2 Margaret Atwood, *MaddAddam* (Toronto, 2013), pp. 140–41; Margaret Atwood, *The Edible Woman* (Toronto, 1969), p. 4;

Margaret Atwood, 'Spotty-Handed Villainesses: Problems of Female Bad Behaviour', in *Curious Pursuits: Occasional Writing* (London, 2005), p. 173.

3 Liane Moriarty, *What Alice Forgot* (Sydney, 2009), p. 367; Liane Moriarty, *The Husband's Secret* (Sydney, 2013), p. 355.

4 Joel Barlow, 'The Hasty-Pudding' (1796), in *American Poetry: The Seventeenth and Eighteenth Centuries*, ed. David S. Shields (New York, 2007), p. 808.

5 Toni Morrison, *Song of Solomon* (New York, 1977), p. 283.

6 Pablo Neruda, *All the Odes: A Bilingual Edition*, ed. Ilan Stavans (New York, 2017), p. 407.

7 Cao Xueqin, *Hung Lo Meng; or, The Dream of the Red Chamber*, vol. 1, trans. H. Bencraft Joly (Hong Kong, 1892), p. 200.

8 See Lisa Yannucci's version on www.mamalisa.com for an English translation and discussion of the song, accessed 15 November 2021.

6 The Future(s) of Breakfast Cereal

1 Centers for Disease Control and Prevention, 'Childhood Overweight and Obesity', www.cdc.gov, accessed 17 October 2021; World Health Organization, 'Obesity', www.who.int, accessed 17 October 2021; U.S. Department of Agriculture and U.S. Department of Health and Human Services, *Dietary Guidelines for Americans, 2020–2025*, 9th edn, December 2020, www.dietaryguidelines.gov, pp. 76, 103.

2 Warren Belasco, *Meals to Come: A History of the Future of Food* (Berkeley, CA, 2006), p. 255.

3 'Love Is in the Bowl: Grape-Nuts Cereal Announces Updated Return Date', Post Consumer Brands, www.postconsumerbrands.com, 11 February 2021.

Select Bibliography

Adichie, Chimamanda Ngozi, *Americanah* (New York, 2013)
Affinita, Antonia, et al., 'Breakfast: A Multidisciplinary
    Approach', *Italian Journal of Pediatrics*, XXXIX/44 (2013)
Anderson, Heather Arndt, *Breakfast: A History* (New York, 2013)
Atwood, Margaret, *The Edible Woman* (Toronto, 1969)
—, *MaddAddam* (Toronto, 2013)
Austen, Jane, *Emma* (London, 1815)
Bauch, Nicholas, *A Geography of Digestion: Biotechnology and the
    Kellogg Cereal Enterprise* (Berkeley, CA, 2017)
Belasco, Warren, *Meals to Come: A History of the Future of Food*
    (Berkeley, CA, 2006)
Boyle, T. C., *The Road to Wellville* (New York, 1993)
Bruce, Scott, and Bill Crawford, *Cerealizing America: The
    Unsweetened Story of American Breakfast Cereal* (Winchester, MA,
    1995)
Carroll, Abigail, *Three Squares: The Invention of the American Meal*
    (New York, 2013)
Carson, Gerald, *Cornflake Crusade* (New York, 1957)
Clausi, Adolph S., Elmer W. Michael and Willard L. Vollink,
    Breakfast Cereal Process, U.S.3121637A, United States Patent
    Office (Washington, DC, 1964)
Collins, E.J.T., 'The "Consumer Revolution" and the Growth
    of Factory Foods: Changing Patterns of Bread and Cereal-
    Eating in Britain in the Twentieth Century', in *The Making
    of the Modern British Diet*, ed. D. S. Miller and D. J. Oddy
    (Totowa, NJ, 1976), pp. 26–43

Dalby, Andrew, *The Breakfast Book* (London, 2013)

Daly, Ed, *Cereal: Snap, Crackle, Pop Culture* (New York, 2011)

Deutsch, Ronald M., *The Nuts Among the Berries* (New York, 1961)

Fayant, Frank, 'The Industry that Cook's the World's Breakfast', *Success*, VI/108 (May 1903), pp. 281–3

Ferdman, Roberto A., 'The Most Popular Breakfast Cereals in America Today', *Washington Post*, www.washingtonpost.com, 18 March 2015

Fussell, Betty, *The Story of Corn: The Myths and History, the Culture and Agriculture, the Art and Science of America's Quintessential Crop* (New York, 1992)

Greenbaum, Hilary, and Dana Rubinstein, 'Who Made That Granola?', *New York Times Magazine*, www.nytimes.com/section/magazine, 23 March 2012

Hollis, Tim, *Part of a Complete Breakfast: Cereal Characters of the Baby Boom Era* (Gainesville, FL, 2012)

Jones, Michael Owen, *Corn: A Global History* (London, 2017)

Kellogg, John Harvey, *Flaked Cereals and Process of Preparing Same*, U.S.558393A, United States Patent Office (Washington, DC, 1896)

Kincaid, Jamaica, 'Biography of a Dress', *Grand Street*, XI (1992), pp. 92–100

Landon, Amanda J., 'The "How" of the Three Sisters: The Origins of Agriculture in Mesoamerica and the Human Niche', *Nebraska Anthropologist*, XL (2008), pp. 110–24

Laudan, Rachel, *Cuisine and Empire: Cooking in World History* (Berkeley, CA, 2013)

McCann, James C., *Stirring the Pot: A History of African Cuisine* (Columbus, OH, 2010)

McGee, Harold, *On Food and Cooking* (New York, 1984)

Markel, Howard, *The Kelloggs: The Battling Brothers of Battle Creek* (New York, 2017)

Marton, Renee, *Rice: A Global History* (London, 2014)

Moriarty, Liane, *What Alice Forgot* (Sydney, 2009)

—, *The Husband's Secret* (Sydney, 2013)

Morrison, Toni, *Song of Solomon* (New York, 1977)

Neruda, Pablo, *All the Odes: A Bilingual Edition*, ed. Ilan Stavans
    (New York, 2017)
Pollan, Michael, *Omnivore's Dilemma* (New York, 2006)
Recinos, Adrián, *Popul Vuh: A Sacred Book of the Ancient Quiché
    Maya*, trans. Delia Goetz and Sylvanus G. Morley (Norman,
    OK, 1950)
Rowling, J. K., *Harry Potter and the Philosopher's Stone* (London,
    1997)
—, *Harry Potter and the Chamber of Secrets* (London, 1998)
Saki (H. H. Munro), *Humor, Horror, and the Supernatural: 22 Stories
    by Saki* (New York, 1977)
Smith, Andrew F., *Eating History: Thirty Turning Points in the
    Making of American Cuisine* (New York, 2009)
—, *Sugar* (London, 2015)
Snyder, Harry, and Charles Woods, 'Cereal Breakfast Foods',
    U.S. *Department of Agriculture Farmers' Bulletin*, no. 249, United
    States Department of Agriculture (Washington, DC, 1906)
Xueqin, Cao, *Hung Lo Meng, or, The Dream of the Red Chamber*,
    trans. H. Bencraft Joly (Hong Kong, 1892)
Zabinski, Catherine, *Amber Waves: The Extraordinary Biography of
    Wheat, from Wild Grass to World Megacrop* (Chicago, IL, 2020)

Websites and Associations

A useful website for general information on breakfast cereal is the *Encyclopaedia Britannica*:

www.britannica.com

A few fun nostalgic websites on breakfast cereal culture are Mr Breakfast, Spoon University and Click Americana:

www.mrbreakfast.com
https://spoonuniversity.com
https://clickamericana.com

The Museum of Food and Drink has an exhibit on the history of the puffing gun and breakfast cereal:

www.mofad.org

Various American and global cereal companies have engaging websites with useful information, recipes and other materials. These include American brands Post Consumer Brands, General Mills, Kellogg's and Quaker Oats, as well as Nestlé and Sanitarium Health Food Company:

www.postconsumerbrands.com
www.generalmills.com
www.kelloggs.com
www.quakeroats.com
www.nestle-cereals.com
www.sanitarium.com.au

Yale University's Rudd Center for Food Policy and Obesity created the website Cereal f.a.c.t.s., and The Cornucopia Institute created a cereal scorecard, both of which are useful for finding breakfast cereal health information:

www.cerealfacts.org
www.cornucopia.org

Cereal-titled and cereal-themed magazines and cultural websites include those of the lifestyle magazines *Porridge* and *Cereal*, New-York food-based artist Sarah Rosado, Greg A. Hill's *Portaging Rideau* cereal-box canoe and Elicser Elliott's cereal-box paintings:

https://porridgemagazine.com
https://readcereal.com
www.sr-artwork.com
https://gregahill.com
www.elicser.com

Breakfast cereal-themed festivals include Scotland's Golden Spurtle porridge-making competition and Battle Creek, Michigan's annual Cereal Fest:

www.goldenspurtle.com
www.bcfestivals.com

Acknowledgements

I would like to thank the editors at Reaktion Books for their kindness and attentiveness as they helped me through the various stages of this book. Thanks to Alex Ciobanu, Susannah Jayes and Amy Salter, and especially to Michael Leaman and Andrew Smith for their valuable comments on earlier drafts of the book. Thanks as well to the librarians at the Stephen O. Murray and Keelung Hong Special Collections at Michigan State University, who assisted me with archival work on the John Harvey Kellogg papers, which contributed to my second chapter: Leslie M. Van Veen McRoberts, Tad Boehmer, Ed Busch, Andrea Salazar McMillan, Jennie Russell, Randall Scott and especially Leslie Behm, as well as the rest of the librarians and staff who assisted me. I was greatly aided with the initial research for an early draft of this manuscript by Lilian Adams during her First Year Research Experience at Missouri University of Science and Technology. In addition, I appreciated the opportunity to present elements of my breakfast cereal research at the Food Studies Knowledge Community conference in Kaohsiung, Taiwan, as well as the Midwest Modern Language Association conference in Chicago, both in 2019. The other conference participants gave thoughtful and perceptive suggestions to my research, often over a meal or a beverage – a great way to do research! Thanks to friends and family for reading earlier drafts and versions of this book over the years. Finally, thank you to my three cats – Oz, Missy and Sammy – for entertaining me (distracting me?) while I wrote!

Photo Acknowledgements

The author and publishers wish to thank the organizations and individuals listed below for authorizing reproduction of their work.

Archive.org: p. 84; Bonhams: p. 9 (Public Domain); The Alan and Shirley Brocker Sliker Collection MSS 314, Special Collections, Michigan State University Libraries: pp. 68 (https://lib.msu.edu/sliker/object/226), 72 (https://lib.msu.edu/sliker/object/249), 73 (https://lib.msu.edu/sliker/object/2585), 76 (https://lib.msu.edu/sliker/object/11427); Kathryn Cornell Dolan: pp. 30, 33, 50, 65, 97, 103, 104; Flickr: p. 58 (Matthew Paul Argall); www.hakes.com/Auction/ItemDetail/224092/FORCE-CEREAL-BOX-PANELS-WITH-SUPERMAN: p. 75; The Historic American Cookbook Project, Michigan State University: p. 43; Rachel Hyland: p. 57; W. K. Kellogg Arabian Horse Library, Special Collections and Archives, University Library, California State Polytechnic University, Pomona: pp. 46, 62, 63 (all: collection no. 0015); Library of Congress, Washington, DC: pp. 36, 39, 48, 70, 88; Metropolitan Museum of Art, New York: pp. 19 (Rogers Fund, 1930), 23 (Gift of Norbert Schimmel, 1985), 24 (The Howard Mansfield Collection, Purchase, Rogers Fund, 1936), 92 (Gift of Theodore De Witt, 1923), 94 (Purchase, Anonymous, Richard, Ann, John, and James Solomon Families Foundation, Adam Lindemann and Amalia Dayan, and Herbert and Lenore Schorr Gifts, Rogers Fund, and funds from various donors, 2013); courtesy of Michigan State University Archives and Historical Collections: p. 42 (Box22N29); courtesy of the Missouri Historical Society: p. 52; Missouri History Museum: p. 77; Nationalmuseum,

Index

italic numbers refer to illustrations; **bold** to recipes